Development of Christian Doctrine

Development of Christian Doctrine
Some Historical Prolegomena

by Jaroslav Pelikan

New Haven and London, Yale University Press, 1969

Library of Congress catalog card number: 69–14864

Designed by Helen Frisk Buzyna,
set in Baskerville type,
and printed in the United States of America by
The Carl Purington Rollins Printing-Office
of the Yale University Press, New Haven, Conn.
Distributed in Great Britain, Europe, Asia, and
Africa by Yale University Press Ltd., London; in
Canada by McGill University Press, Montreal; and
in Latin America by Centro Interamericano de Libros
Académicos, Mexico City.

To
Gustave Weigel, S.J.
(1906–1964)
and
John Courtney Murray, S.J.
(1904–1967)
in fond and fraternal memory

Preface

This book contains the St. Thomas More Lectures which I delivered at Yale in the autumn of 1965 under the general theme, "Doctrinal Development and Catholic Unity." In revised form, those lectures constitute the third, fourth, and fifth chapters. But I was urged by several hearers and readers—above all, by the late John Courtney Murray, S.J., into whose hands I had hoped to place the first copy of this book—to balance the detailed analysis in those historical chapters with a more general theological discussion of approximately equal length, putting my patristic research into the context of the problem of development of doctrine.

Thus when Father Murray and his colleagues at Woodstock College invited me to deliver the first Gustave Weigel Memorial Lecture, also in 1965, it was suggested that I set forth the rationale for patristic scholarship as a means of dealing with that problem. In the same year I devoted my presidential address at the American Society of Church History to the role of historical study in the examination of doctrinal development. These two presentations are here combined to form the second chapter. Again at Father Murray's invitation, I prepared a critique of the historical conclusions in Leslie Dewart's widely-discussed *The Future of Belief* for publication first as a review article in *Theological Studies,* of which Father Murray was editor, and then as part of the first chapter in this book. And to provide an overall account of how doctrinal development has become, in Father Murray's words, the place where "the parting of the ways between the two Christian communities takes place," I have opened my theological discussion with the revised form of an earlier analysis, originally presented at St. John's University in Collegeville, Minnesota, of Cardinal Newman's *An Essay on the Development of Christian Doctrine* as an epitome of the polemical encounter between Roman Catholicism and Protestantism.

My debt to John Courtney Murray is therefore evident throughout the volume. Also important, though quite different in both a personal and a scholarly way, is my debt to the late Gustave Weigel, S.J. Not only did my reading of the manuscript of his 1960 foreword to a new edition of the *Essay on Development* direct my attention once more to that seminal work, but in our conversations and correspondence during the following years we found that development of doctrine was the issue at which he, as a Roman Catholic dogmatic theologian, and I, as a Lutheran historian of dogma, could meet and debate most profitably. To those debates I owe much of my awareness, evidenced I hope in the chapters of this book, both of the subtle connections between theological thought and historical scholarship and of the often more subtle disjunctions between them. It therefore seemed appropriate to name Father Murray and Father Weigel together in my dedication, and it is my privilege to do so.

My thanks are due as well to many others: to the St. Thomas More House at Yale University and to its chaplain, Father James T. Healy, Jr., for generously inviting me to give the St. Thomas More Lectures; to my audiences at the lectures, for their questions and criticisms; to the libraries

of Yale, whose unmatched holdings gave me access not only
to the standard works of my field, both primary and secondary, but to the Newman materials and the other rare books
cited; to Newman Press, Herder and Herder, *Theological
Studies* and *Church History,* for permission to quote my-
self; to my secretary and editorial assistant, Mrs. Margaret
Schulze, who typed the successive drafts of the manuscript,
read the proofs, and prepared the index; to various readers
and critics, whose observations have compelled me to clarify
arguments; and to the Yale University Press.

Unless otherwise identified, translations are my own.

J. P.

Yale University
February 1968

Contents

Contents

Abbreviations

CC, SL	*Corpus Christianorum, Series Latina* (Turnhout and Paris, 1953 ff.).
CSCO	*Corpus Scriptorum Christianorum Orientalium* (Louvain and Washington, 1903 ff.).
CSEL	*Corpus Scriptorum Ecclesiasticorum Latinorum* (Vienna, 1866 ff.).
GCS	*Die griechischen christlichen Schriftsteller* (Leipzig and Berlin, 1897 ff.).
PG	*Patrologia Graeca,* ed. J. P. Migne (Paris, 1857–66).
PL	*Patrologia Latina,* ed. J. P. Migne (Paris, 1844–64).

Introduction

I consider that the parting of the ways between the two Christian communities [Roman Catholicism and Protestantism] takes place on the issue of development of doctrine. That development has taken place in both communities cannot possibly be denied. The question is, what is legitimate development, what is organic growth in the understanding of the original deposit of faith, what is warranted extension of the primitive discipline of the Church, and what, on the other hand, is accretion, additive increment, adulteration of the deposit, distortion of true Christian discipline? The question is, what are the valid dynamisms of development and what are the forces of distortion? The question is, what are the criteria by which to judge between healthy and morbid development, between true growth and rank excrescence? The question is, what is archaism and what is futurism? Perhaps, above all, the question is, what are the limits of development and growth—the limits that must be reached on peril of archaistic stuntedness, and the limits that must not be transgressed on peril of futuristic decadence?[1]

In these words the first of the St. Thomas More Lecturers, the late John Courtney Murray, S.J., raised an issue to

1. John Courtney Murray, *The Problem of God: Yesterday and Today* (New Haven, 1964), p. 53.

1

which he was, alas, not granted the opportunity to devote himself as he had intended. Thus it seems appropriate that the first non-Roman Catholic incumbent of the lectureship should take up this issue of development of doctrine. The title of this book, the theme of its first chapter, and a significant part of the *Fragestellung* to which each of its remaining chapters is addressed, all come from John Henry Cardinal Newman's *An Essay on the Development of Christian Doctrine*. Anselm Atkins has said of it: "Not counting pale anticipations in Tertullian's late Montanist works, the first contribution to the theory of development of doctrine was Cardinal Newman's *Essay* of 1845."[2] This judgment is, however, something of an exaggeration, for the *Commonitorium* of Vincent of Lérins was more than a "pale anticipation"; and the late date and rapid emergence of the orthodox doctrine of the Holy Spirit did provide the occasion for Gregory of Nazianzus in the fourth century, for Thomas Aquinas in the thirteenth century, and for some other theologians long before 1845 to comment on doctrinal development both as a phenomenon and as a problem. Yet their comments are of interest primarily as a foil for Newman's *Essay*. It was Newman, moreover, who identified the problem of development of doctrine as the point at which, in Father Murray's words, "the parting of the ways between the two Christian communities takes place."

There was good existential reason for Newman to be aware of this at the time, for it was while the *Essay* was at the printer's that he "recognized in himself a conviction of the truth of the conclusion to which the discussion leads, so

2. Anselm Atkins, "Religious Assertions and Doctrinal Development," *Theological Studies*, 27 (1966), 539.

clear as to supersede further deliberation."[3] Not only the subjective statement of the difficulties raised by the problem of doctrinal development for an Anglican contemplating a change to Roman Catholicism, but also the objective statement of the importance of the problem for the *status controversiae* between Roman Catholicism and other branches of Christendom makes Newman's *Essay* the almost inevitable starting point for an investigation of development of doctrine. But this is not to be yet another book about Cardinal Newman: he is not the subject of it, only the provocation for it.

Part One of this book analyzes the problem of development of doctrine as a theological and scholarly issue, narrowing it down by a series of concentric circles first to the historical investigation of development, and then from this to the exploration of doctrinal development in patristic theology. The opening chapter uses Newman's "tests" of authenticity to specify the locus of the issue of development in the polemical impasse between Protestant and Roman Catholic theology. Yet because in the past decade or so doctrinal development has been debated as vigorously among Roman Catholic theologians themselves as it has between them and Protestant theologians, this chapter also includes a critique of the most widely discussed, if not the most persuasively argued, recent presentation of the question of development by a Roman Catholic thinker. But

3. John Henry Newman, *An Essay on the Development of Christian Doctrine* (1st ed. London, 1845), p. x. Henceforth I shall refer to this work as Newman, *Essay,* meaning the first edition except where (as, for example, p. 73, n. 1) a later edition is being cited. For a recent interpretation of the place of the *Essay* in Newman's own development, see William Robbins, *The Newman Brothers: An Essay in Comparative Intellectual Biography* (Cambridge, Mass., 1966), pp. 102–07.

most of the debate, both between and within the separated communities, has been carried on by theologians who ask the questions catalogued by Father Murray in the paragraph just quoted.

Legitimate though such questions are and unavoidable though they ultimately become, it seems precipitate to launch into a full-length argument about them in the absence of careful historical analysis of how Christian doctrine has in fact developed. The second chapter makes the case for such a posteriori analysis as a necessary prolegomenon to the specification of "a priori principles of development."[4] In the history of the development of doctrine, moreover, the study of the church fathers holds pride of place, both because of the intrinsic importance of the subject matter and because of the controversy it has evoked. Chapter 2 goes on to show that it is proper for patristic research to hold this place in the historical study of development of doctrine, and that the history of such research is itself an encouraging instance of how historical scholarship can transcend confessional bias.

Part Two is devoted to three case studies of the problem of doctrinal development in patristic theology. Although other topics might conceivably have been studied with equal profit, several criteria have converged in the selection of these particular doctrines and theologians. In each case, there is a lacuna in existing scholarship on this man's view

4. Karl Rahner, "Zur Frage der Dogmenentwicklung," *Schriften zur Theologie* (Einsiedeln, 1964 ff.), *1* 49–90; and "Ueberlegungen zur Dogmenentwicklung," ibid., *4*, 11–50, esp. 16–20: "Apriorische Rahmengesetze für die Dogmenentwicklung." Cf. Robert L. Richard, "Rahner's Theory of Doctrinal Development," *Proceedings of the Eighteenth Annual Convention, Catholic Theological Society of America* (1963), pp. 157–89.

of this doctrine; in each case, this theologian appears to have been the first to develop this doctrine *in extenso;* in each case, the doctrine went on to become the officially acknowledged dogma of the Church or, more precisely, of part of the Church; in each case, doctrinal development has also become an issue between one Christian tradition and another. Thus the dogma of original sin, treated in the third chapter, is in some sense the universal possession of all Christians who claim to be orthodox, but the legitimacy of the development of this dogma has in fact been debated between Eastern Orthodoxy and Roman Catholicism as well as within Protestantism. The process by which it developed in the first century of Latin theology, even before its full statement by Augustine, is therefore an important part of the history of the developemnt of doctrine.

Chapter 4 turns to the dogma over which much of the battle about doctrinal development has been fought, the doctrine of Mary. It examines the development of mariology not in the theologians of the Latin West, where, during our own century, it has achieved a new dogmatic status, but in those of the Greek East, and specifically in Athanasius, who is acknowledged by Latin, Greek, and Syriac Christianity, as well as by mainstream Protestantism, with such honorific titles as "father of orthodoxy."[5]

Not at all acknowledged as orthodox by Greek and Syriac Christianity is the Filioque, whose origins are described in the fifth chapter, the doctrine of the procession of the Holy Spirit "ex Patre Filioque," from both the Father and the Son. Together with the mariology analyzed in the preceding chapter, the Filioque illustrates how the theological

5. See, for example, Gregory of Nazianzus, *Orationes* xxi, "In laudem magni Athanasii episcopi Alexandrini," *PG 35,* 1081–128.

controversies between the various Christian traditions often come down to the question of development of dogma. Hilary, whose doctrine of Filioque is exposed here, stands in an especially interesting position between the traditions. For it was Hilary who, more than anyone else, caught up the trinitarian development of the Greek-speaking East and transmitted it to the Latin-speaking West,[6] especially to Augustine and then to Boethius, in the form in which these two thinkers in turn transmitted it to subsequent Western theology, as can be seen, for example, in the *Expositio et quaestiones in librum Boethii de Trinitate* of Thomas Aquinas.[7] The physiology of doctrinal development set forth in these three chapters does not claim to exhaust the list of developmental processes, but it does isolate some of the more interesting ones for closer diagnosis.

6. Cf. P. Löffler, "Die Trinitätslehre des Bischofs Hilarius von Poitiers zwischen Ost und West," *Zeitschrift für Kirchengeschichte, 71* (1960), 26–36; and Gustave Bardy, "Traducteurs et adapteurs au IVe siècle," *Recherches de science religieuse, 30* (1940), 257–306.

7. A critical edition of this treatise, on which the present writer is collaborating, is to appear in the new edition of the works of Thomas Aquinas being published by the Leonine Commission.

Part One

The Problem of
Doctrinal Development

I
The State of
The Problem

Ever since the Reformation, theologians have been trying to identify the issues that divide Roman Catholics and Protestants as well as the convictions that unite them. Some of the issues that originally divided the two communities are no longer as relevant to their divisions as they used to be. The reinterpretation of the theology of Luther and Calvin by Protestant scholarship during the past two generations and the corresponding reinterpretation of the doctrinal decrees of the Council of Trent by Roman Catholic scholarship have changed the thought of both sides about the precise nature of their differences.[1]

Previous generations identified the doctrine of justification by faith alone *(sola fide)* and the doctrine of the authority of the Bible alone *(sola Scriptura)* as "the formal principle" and "the material principle" of the Reformation and thus as the central points at issue between the two communities.[2] Even though the nomenclature was mooted,[3]

1. Cf. Wilhelm Pauck, "The Historiography of the German Reformation During the Past Twenty Years," *Church History*, 9 (1940), 305–40; Edward A. Dowey, Jr., "Continental Reformation: Works of General Interest. Studies in Calvin and Calvinism Since 1955," *Church History*, 29 (1960), 187–204; and George H. Tavard, "The Catholic Reform in the Sixteenth Century," *Church History*, 26 (1957), 275–88.

2. See, for example, Julius Köstlin, *The Theology of Luther in its Historical Development and Inner Harmony*, trans. Charles E. Hay (2 vols. Philadelphia, 1897), *1*, 208–09.

3. Cf. Philip Hefner, *Faith and the Vitalities of History: A Theological*

the importance of these two doctrines was generally accepted. Yet several studies of the doctrine of justification have led to the conclusion that the divergence between the doctrine decreed at Trent and the doctrine taught by Protestants may have been overstated.[4] Much to his surprise, Karl Barth found that Hans Küng had managed to harmonize the Barthian restatement of the Reformation doctrine of justification with the formulation of the sixth session of the Council of Trent.[5]

The principle of *sola Scriptura,* too, can no longer be considered divisive in the same way that it once was. Many Roman Catholics concede that the post-biblical tradition of the Church is not to be regarded as a second source of revelation alongside Scripture, but only as the process by which a revelation contained completely in Scripture is being made explicit; and they are trying to prove that the Tridentine decrees at least did not exclude this position.[6] Meanwhile, Protestants concede that there was a Christian tradition before there was a New Testament, and that the subsequent interpretation of the New Testament has been

---

Study Based on the Work of Albrecht Ritschl, Makers of Modern Theology, ed. Jaroslav Pelikan (New York, 1966), pp. 54–58.

4. Hans Küng, *Justification: The Doctrine of Karl Barth and a Catholic Reflection, with a Letter by Karl Barth,* trans. Thomas Collins, Edmund E. Tolk, and David Granskou (New York, 1964); also the work of Pesch, cited on p. 55, n. 49 below.

5. Küng, pp. xix–xxii.

6. Cf. Josef Rupert Geiselmann, "Scripture, Tradition, and the Church: An Ecumenical Problem," in Daniel J. Callahan, Heiko A. Oberman, and Daniel J. O'Hanlon, eds., *Christianity Divided* (New York, 1961), pp. 39–72; but see also Newman, *Essay,* p. 320.

shaped by the ongoing tradition of the Church.[7] Both the doctrine of justification by faith and the doctrine of the authority of the Bible are vastly more complex than this terse summary would suggest, but for the purposes of this book it is sufficient to note that very few participants in the present discussions between Protestantism and Roman Catholicism would find it possible to treat these doctrines as they were treated in the sixteenth century.

On the other hand, some of the shared convictions that underlay the controversies of the sixteenth century are not shared any longer.[8] Luther believed in the perpetual virginity of Mary and continued to affirm it all his life.[9] During the centuries since the Reformation, Roman Catholicism has gone far beyond the dogma of the perpetual virginity to affirm the immaculate conception of the Blessed Virgin Mary and her bodily assumption into heaven, while a great many Protestants have gone on to deny not only the perpetual virginity of Mary but the virgin birth of Jesus Christ as well. Similarly, modern Protestant theology and biblical criticism have recast the theological doctrine of the person of Christ so basically that the agreement between the principal Reformers of the sixteenth century and their Roman Catholic opponents on the christological consensus

7. Albert C. Outler, *The Christian Tradition and the Unity We Seek* (New York, 1957).

8. See the comments, partly autobiograpical, of Gustave Weigel, "Protestantism as a Catholic Concern," *Theological Studies, 16* (1955), 214–32.

9. On the mariology of Luther, cf., for example, his sermon of January 19, 1538, *Luther's Works*, American Edition, ed. Jaroslav Pelikan and Helmut L. Lehmann (St. Louis and Philadelphia, 1955 ff.), 22, 214–15, and my note there.

of the Councils of Ephesus and Chalcedon can no longer be taken for granted as a basis for discussion.

For four hundred years now Roman Catholicism and Protestantism have had separate histories, during which they have both undergone changes. One of the primary assignments for any ecumenical discussion must be a kind of theological cartography, to determine where the present boundaries actually lie.

NEWMAN'S CRITERIA OF AUTHENTICITY

For such an assignment, the problem of development of doctrine is perhaps the most useful point of organization. Even more than the related problem of authority, doctrinal development may be seen as the question at issue between Roman Catholic dogma and the several theological positions within Protestantism. For example, it is possible to categorize the various stands of Christian groups and thinkers on the significance of the Virgin Mary as theological counterparts to the various stages in the historical development of mariology.[10] The several positions may thus be identified by the point up to which they regard the development as authoritative, between the earliest reference to her, the formula "born of woman" in Galatians 4:4 (which all Christians accept, even the most antitraditional), and the most recent, the apostolic constitution *Munificentissimus Deus* of Pope Pius XII (which only Roman Catholics accept).

Whether or not this interpretation of mariological doctrine holds, it is clear that the problem of development in doctrine is fundamental among the issues that divide Roman

10. Jaroslav Pelikan, "Mary, the Mother of Jesus," *Encyclopaedia Britannica* (1968 ed.), *14*, 990–92.

Catholics and Protestants—indeed, fundamental to most of the other issues that divide them. Because Newman's *Essay on Development* is the classic discussion of doctrinal development, his seven tests proposed as criteria for distinguishing authentic development in Christian doctrine from doctrinal corruption, confused and overlapping though they often are, are also convenient points around which to group Protestant theories about doctrinal development.

The Preservation of Type or Idea

One of the differences between heresy and the Church, according to Newman, was the "fecundity of the heretical principle.... [which] was, by its very nature, its own master, free to change, self-sufficient; and, having thrown off the yoke of the Church, it was little likely to submit to any usurped and spurious authority."[11] By contrast, any development in the Catholic Church had to preserve the basic type or idea of the Church. Therefore, it was "almost a note of the Church, for the use of the most busy and the most ignorant, that she was on one side and all other bodies on the other."[12] Thus catholicity was said to be a mark that distinguished the Church from heresy and genuine development from corruption. For heresies and sects did not preserve the type, but were named according to their founders or their special provenance, while the Church was universal and its developments preserved the original type or idea of the Church.

Protestants have usually denied both the theological and the historical implications of the claim that the develop-

11. Newman, *Essay,* pp. 246–47.
12. Ibid., p. 428.

ments of Roman Catholic Christianity have in fact preserved the type or idea. In various ways and with varying
degrees of radicalism, Protestants have asserted "the fall of
the Church," i.e. the defection of the doctrinal development
from its type or norm. Luther could not decide when it had
happened, whether before, during, or after the pontificate
of Gregory I.[13] More radical Protestants have dated the fall
much earlier.[14] Those who have stressed the antithesis between the Church and the world have generally identified it
with the Constantinian settlement.[15] Those whose criticism
has been directed against the authority of the episcopate
or the rise of dogma have traced the apostasy to the second
or the third century.[16] Sebastian Franck spoke for the most
radical Protestantism of all when he said that "right after
the death of the apostles [the Church] went up into heaven
and lies concealed in the Spirit and in truth."[17] In this
radical view the development of a Catholic Church with
bishops, creed, and canon was seen as a corruption of the
normative type or idea of apostolic Christianity. This is an
issue that does divide some Protestants from other Protestants, but it also divides all Protestants from all Roman
Catholics.

13. Cf. John M. Headley, *Luther's View of Church History* (New Haven,
1963), pp. 187–92.

14. See Franklin Hamlin Littell, *The Origins of Sectarian Protestantism:
A Study of the Anabaptist view of the Church* (New York, 1964), pp. 46–78:
"The Fall of the Church."

15. For a modern version, cf. G. J. Heering, *The Fall of Christianity*, trans.
J. W. Thompson (London, 1930), pp. 54–62.

16. Littell, pp. 67–70.

17. "A Letter to John Campanus by Sebastian Franck, Strassburg, 1531,"
Spiritual and Anabaptist Writers, ed. George Huntston Williams, The Library of Christian Classics (Philadelphia, 1957), p. 149; cf. pp. 152–53, where

Continuity of Principles

No interpretation of doctrinal development merits serious consideration unless it comes to terms with the stubborn fact of the doctrinal variety within every age of church history and between one age and another. Newman's explanation of this doctrinal variety was called forth by a judgment of the French historian, François Guizot: "The first Christians assembled to enjoy together the same emotions, the same religious convictions. We do not find any doctrinal system established, any form of discipline or of laws, or any body of magistrates."[18] In reply to this effort to relegate doctrine to an unimportant position, Newman maintained that amid all the variety of doctrinal formulations characteristic of the ante-Nicene Church, for example, one could still discern a continuity of principles. Thus the early period of the Church's history "was the age of Martyrs, of acting not of thinking. Doctors succeeded Martyrs, as light and peace of conscience follow upon obedience to it; yet, even before the Church had grown into the full measure of its doctrines, it was rooted in its principles."[19] The authenticity of a doctrinal development was therefore to be decided on the basis of its fidelity to these continuing principles, despite the admitted variety manifested by the development as a whole.

Many Protestants would warmly applaud the proposition that the continuity of the Church is not in its dogmatics. But they would side with Guizot against Newman—or perhaps

---

Franck rejects the idea that the fall of the Church did not occur until the time of Constantine.

18. François Pierre Guizot, *European Civilization*, pp. 56–58, quoted in Newman, *Essay*, p. 58.

19. Newman, *Essay*, p. 348.

with the Newman of the *Grammar of Assent* against the Newman of the *Essay on Development*—and locate the continuity not in "principles" but in the Christian experience. In a very sophisticated version of this argument, Friedrich Schleiermacher, demonstrating affinities with Newman that are more than casual,[20] argued that a description of the meaning of the Christian faith could be "taken from the realm of inner experience, and that therefore in this form nothing alien can creep into the system of Christian doctrine."[21] It was necessary, he admitted, for theology to use other forms of expression as means of establishing its historical and ecclesiastical continuity and of presenting its credentials; but the basic form, to which these others were to be subordinated, remained the experiential. Accordingly, a doctrinal development was authentic if it could demonstrate its congruence with inner experience. By "experience," Schleiermacher—and, a fortiori, Newman—did not mean the undifferentiated and idiosyncratic emotions of each individual Christian. Schleiermacher saw this "experience" in the setting of the Church—its memory, its witness, its celebration.[22] And the continuity of the Christian faith despite doctrinal variety he professed to see in this experience, not in principles, for these were themselves derived from experience.

20. Cf. J. H. Walgrave, *Newman the Theologian: The Nature of Belief and Doctrine as Exemplified in His Life and Works,* trans. A. V. Littledale (New York, 1960), pp. 71–92, 334–41.

21. Friedrich Schleiermacher, *The Christian Faith,* trans. H. R. Mackintosh and J. S. Stewart (Edinburgh, 1956), p. 126.

22. Cf. Gerhard Spiegler, *The Eternal Covenant: Schleiermacher's Experiment in Cultural Theology,* Makers of Modern Theology, ed. Jaroslav Pelikan (New York, 1967), pp. 136–56.

Assimilative Power

Schleiermacher's reference to "alien" elements that "creep into the system of Christian doctrine" suggests that the extra-Christian sources of Christian thought raise serious difficulties for any definition of what constitutes legitimate doctrinal development. How can Christian doctrinal development be regarded as pure or true if it has borrowed from the very systems of pagan thought against which Christian doctrinal development has defined itself? Newman stood this argument on its head. He acknowledged the borrowing from extra-Christian sources and pointed to the Church's assimilation of them as proof of its power. Christians, he argued, could trace many of these "alien" elements to primitive revelation and could see in them "shadows" for which the Church possessed the "archetypes." Therefore the "instruments and appendages of demon-worship" could be adapted to an "evangelical use." In this confidence "the rulers of the Church from early times were prepared, should the occasion arise, to adopt, or imitate, or sanction the existing rites and customs of the populace as well as the philosophy of the educated class."[23] Far from invalidating the Christian developments for which it was responsible, this power of assimilation helped to authenticate them.

The most influential Protestant research into the relation between Christian theology and its sources in extra-Christian thought has probably been that of the distinguished historian of dogma, Adolf von Harnack. Both his historical study and his theological presuppositions made Harnack think otherwise about the power of assimiliation. The syn-

23. Newman, *Essay,* p. 358.

cretism of the Gnostics, for instance, was the extreme form of a syncretism that he claimed to discern within the Church itself: "In Gnosticism there is represented the acute outcome of a process which began even earlier in the Church and which underwent a slow and specific development in the Catholic system," that is, the process of hellenization.[24] Going even further than Harnack,[25] the historical relativism propounded by the *religionsgeschichtliche Schule* of biblical and historical research has interpreted early Christianity as a combination of elements, and has demanded, on this basis as well as on others, that Christianity surrender its claim to ultimacy.[26] Although the prestige of this school has declined in the scholarship of recent decades, its presence is still visible in the continuing attention of historical theology to the problem of the evolution of doctrine in relation to the non-Christian environment of the Church. The prevailing mood of Protestant theology today may oppose Harnack's theological liberalism, but as represented by Karl Barth, it is, if anything, even more hostile than he was to the idea of assimilation.

24. Adolf von Harnack, [*Grundriss der*] *Dogmengeschichte* (4th ed. Tübingen, 1905), p. 56.
25. "As a result of their romantic bias toward what is primitive and of their inflated *Formgeschichte*," Harnack predicted in 1921, "true interest in ancient church history can go to the devil in one generation." Quoted in Agnes von Zahn-Harnack, *Adolf von Harnack* (2d ed. Berlin, 1951), p. 401. On Harnack's conflict with the *religionsgeschichtliche Schule*, see G. Wayne Glick, *The Reality of Christianity: A Study of Adolf von Harnack as Historian and Theologian*, Makers of Modern Theology, ed. Jaroslav Pelikan (New York, 1967), pp. 209–15.
26. Karl Holl, "Urchristentum und Religionsgeschichte," *Gesammelte Aufsätze zur Kirchengeschichte*, Vol. 2: *Der Osten* (Tübingen, 1928), 1–32, is a scholarly answer to this position.

Early Anticipation

The criteria of preservation, continuity, and assimilation all raise the question of authenticity in relation to the deposit of original Christian revelation. How can a development claim to be authentic unless it can be supported by explicit reference to the Bible? Newman found it necessary "to determine whether certain developments, which did afterwards and do exist, have not sufficient countenance in early times, that we may pronounce them to be true developments and not corruptions."[27] From the specific doctrinal issues to which Newman applied this criterion and from his earlier discussion of the authority of Scripture, it is clear what he meant to say: Scripture must be said to contain implicitly the doctrines that the later doctrinal development of the Church has made explicit in creed and dogmatic decree. Thus it was not necessary to contend that the writer of the protevangel in Genesis 3:15 was expressing everything that later development has found in the passage, but it was necessary to see a posteriori that the promise of "the seed of the woman" anticipated what the Church came eventually to teach both about the Seed and about the Woman.[28]

Not Cardinal Newman but the fourth session of the Council of Trent has usually been the provocation for Protestant declarations on this subject. Commenting on its decrees, Martin Chemnitz acknowledged that there were traditions apart from the Scriptures and that these deserved the serious attention of Christians. But he objected to the Tridentine formulation because "the Council of Trent attributes to un-

27. Newman, *Essay*, p. 388.
28. Cf. B. Rigaux, "La Femme et son lignage dans Genèse III, 14–15," *Revue biblique, 61* (1954), 321–48.

written traditions pertaining to both faith and morals a right to the same reverence and piety as Sacred Scripture itself."[29] Chemnitz was speaking here for most of the Protestant tradition in asserting *sola Scriptura* over against the decrees of Trent on Scripture, tradition, and traditions. Yet *sola Scriptura* has not meant the same to all Protestants. Historical examination of how the Reformers used tradition in their exegesis has qualified both their own statements about *sola Scriptura* as a principle and the construction put upon this principle by later interpreters.[30]

Logical Sequence

Newman claimed to be able to identify "the mind of the Church working out dogmatic truths from implicit feelings under secret supernatural guidance."[31] Two controverted doctrines in whose development he discerned this process were the doctrine of Mary and the doctrine of purgatory. Both of them were logical conclusions to be drawn from other doctrines and principles already accepted by the Church. Newman insisted that he who said *homoousios* with Nicaea had to go on to say *Theotokos* with Ephesus. "In order to do honour to Christ, in order to defend the true doctrine of the Incarnation, in order to secure a right faith in the manhood of the Eternal Son, the Council of Ephesus determined the Blessed Virgin to be the Mother of God."[32]

29. Martin Chemnitz, *Examen Concilii Tridentini*, quoted in Jaroslav Pelikan, *Obedient Rebels: Catholic Substance and Protestant Principle in Luther's Reformation* (New York, 1964), pp. 49–53.

30. Cf. Jaroslav Pelikan, *Luther the Expositor: Introduction to the Reformer's Exegetical Writings* (St. Louis, 1959), pp. 48–88.

31. Newman, *Essay*, p. 417.

32. Ibid., p. 407.

Thus a development was authentic if it stood in a systematic connection with other previous developments, forming one whole with them or being deducible from them. As the presence of an invisible planet could be established from the charting of a solar system, so the composition of the doctrinal system could validate what appeared to be a new doctrine by demonstrating its necessary place in the logical sequence.

Luther's objection to this method of constructing Christian doctrine was one of the most important arguments in his attack on the scholastic theology of the late Middle Ages. His *Disputation Against Scholastic Theology* of 1517 formulated this attack in a succession of theses: "To state that a theologian who is not a logician is a monstrous heretic— this is a monstrous and heretical statement. . . . In vain does one fashion a logic of faith. . . . No syllogistic form is valid when applied to divine terms."[33] In some ways this has been the obverse side of the principle of a *sola Scriptura*. The proper method of establishing a doctrine as Christian was to show its scriptural source, not to locate it in the structure of a system of doctrine. If a doctrine could be found in Scripture and could not be accommodated to a system, even to the Church's system, the doctrine had to stand nevertheless; and if some idea fit the system but had no biblical warrant, it was at best entitled to the status of a private theologoumenon, but not to that of a Christian doctrine.

Preservative Additions

All the tests considered thus far have sought to deal with the additions that the history of the Church has made to its

33. Martin Luther, *Disputation Against Scholastic Theology*, Theses 45–47, *Luther's Works, 31*, 12.

original doctrines. The attacks upon these additions have provoked the Church's defense. "It is," wrote Newman,

> the general pretext of heretics that they are but serving and protecting Christianity by their innovations; and it is their charge against what by this time we may surely call the Catholic Church, that her successive definitions of doctrine have but overlaid and obscured it.[34]

In Newman's conversion, at least as documented in the *Essay on Development,* the implications of this criterion appear to have played a decisive role. He finally found it impossible to follow the pattern of Anglicanism, that is, to accept the trinitarian and christological dogmas of the ancient Church without accepting the ecclesiological precondition of those dogmas, the authority of Rome; for the precondition seemed to be better authenticated in the early Church than were such ancient dogmas as the Trinity or original sin. These dogmas or additions were preservative of that faith which the Church had been confessing all along. How could one be loyal to the dogmas without also being obedient to the Church?

The answer of Protestant orthodoxy to this question was to assert that the dogmas were merely summaries of scriptural doctrine and that the role of the Church in their formulation had been a purely passive one. Even in confessional orthodoxy, which demanded subscription to creeds, the assertion was made that the dogmatic additions to the faith were not substantive. "The Church requires subscription to the doctrines contained in her creeds and confessions, not because they are in the creeds and confessions but be-

---

34. Newman, *Essay,* p. 428.

cause they are in Scripture."[35] There has therefore been no doctrinal development. Indeed, "there cannot be a development of Christian doctrine, because Christian doctrine is an entity that was completely closed with the doctrine of the apostles, which is not to be developed in the course of time, but to be preserved and taught utterly without change."[36] Additions were not preservative but destructive of doctrinal truth, by the very definition of Christian doctrine.

Chronic Continuance

Newman's final criterion, and the one least developed in his *Essay*, was that of chronic continuance. The sheer duration of the Church and of its life helped to argue for the authenticity of its doctrinal developments. "The integrity of the Catholic developments," Newman wrote, "is still more evident when they are viewed in contrast with the history of other doctrinal systems," that is, with "philosophies and religions of the world." In contrast with them, "the Catholic religion alone has had no limits; it alone has ever been greater than the emergence, and can do what others cannot do."[37] Newman did not mean to argue that continuance proved the Church's case incontestably, but it did lend support to other arguments.

Even in this form, however, the argument from chronic continuance has met with Protestant opposition from various quarters. Harnack maintained that "church history shows in its very beginnings that 'primitive Christianity' had to disappear so that 'Christianity' might remain; and

35. Franz Pieper, *Christliche Dogmatik, I* (St. Louis, 1924), 427.
36. Ibid., p. 148.
37. Newman, *Essay*, p. 449.

thus in later ages one metamorphosis followed another."[38] Contemporary theologians in Protestantism, notably those with an existentialist orientation, stress discontinuity even more radically. They interpret the Church as coming into being when the Word is preached, not necessarily as continuing between the times of its appearance. From some such premise Gerhard Ebeling has urged that the history of the Church be read as the history of biblical interpretation.[39] Chronic continuance is an argument against, not for, the authenticity of the doctrinal developments in the Church.

The nineteenth and twentieth centuries have been preeminently the age of historical study in theology. They have therefore been the time when the problem of doctrinal development has forced itself increasingly upon the attention of theologians. Most of the principal reactions of Protestant theology to the problem of development have at the same time involved the Protestant attitude toward Roman Catholicism, even though the problem has often been raised by secular or Protestant historical scholarship rather than by Roman Catholic views of the living magisterium. A study of how Protestants interpret the problem of development is simultaneously a study of how they understand their relation to Roman Catholic thought. And contemporary discussions of questions like Scripture, tradition, and papal infallibility may well begin by a reconsideration of what development has meant in the history of the Church—and in the histories of the churches.

38. Adolf von Harnack, *Das Wesen des Christentums* (4th ed. Leipzig, 1901), p. 9.
39. Gerhard Ebeling, *Kirchengeschichte als Geschichte der Auslegung der Heiligen Schrift* (Tübingen, 1947).

DEWART'S HISTORICAL CONCLUSIONS

Recent theological discussion, however, has drastically altered the map drawn by traditional cartographers. The most radical questions raised by the most radical Protestant theologians and historians are now being asked by Roman Catholic thinkers in the years since the Second Vatican Council. Among these thinkers, one of the most widely discussed has been Leslie Dewart. His book, *The Future of Belief*,[40] is an essay about the future addressed by a philosopher to theologians, and it deserves first of all to be read as such. Nevertheless, it embodies certain judgments about the past that have direct implications for the historical study of the development of Christian doctrine. For while "the retelling of the whole history of Christian dogma from the apostolic age until our own day" is not its purpose, it does purport to be based on "the conclusion[s] of historical research."[41] At least three of these conclusions seem to require comment within the context of this examination of the problem of development.

The Hellenization of Christianity

Professor Dewart explicitly dissociates his interpretation of "hellenism" from that of Harnack, on the grounds that Harnack thought of the process of hellenization as a corruption while Dewart thinks of it as a stage of development once useful but no longer relevant. Thus he calls for "dehelleni-

---

40. Leslie Dewart, *The Future of Belief* (New York, 1966). Cf. Gregory Baum, ed., *The Future of Belief Debate* (New York, 1967).
41. Dewart, p. 132.

zation of dogma, and specifically that of the Christian doctrine of God" as his program.[42] What is the content of this hellenism? Dewart includes such notions as "the hellenic principle that man's perfection *is* happiness," "the hellenic philosophical viewpoint" that equates "intelligibility and necessity," "a hellenic idea that development must be reducible to becoming," "the presumed truth of God's self-identity, which is a hellenization of the Christian experience."[43] This "hellenization of Christian philosophical speculation . . . [constitutes], in point of historical fact, the condition of the possibility of modern atheism."[44] Applied to the doctrine of God, hellenism brought it about that God was "fittingly conceived as a suprarational person," and it was in this way responsible for the doctrine of the Trinity.[45] Analyzing the development of Christian dogmatic language, Dewart states that early Christianity could not "have created the concepts whereby to elaborate itself." Instead, it did the only thing it could do, which "was to use the concepts of which it was *already* possessed." And so he summarizes the development of dogma as follows: "The intellectual effort of the early centuries was, therefore, predominantly directed to the adaptation of hellenic conceptions to serve the

42. Ibid., pp. 133, 49; on Harnack's view of hellenization, cf. Glick, pp. 150–52. See also Aloys Grillmeier, "Hellenisierung-Judaisierung des Christentums als Deutprinzipien der Geschichte des kirchlichen Dogmas," *Scholastik, 33* (1958), 321–55, 528–58.

43. Dewart, pp. 32, 44, 74.

44. Ibid., p. 153.

45. Ibid., p. 187; Werner Elert, on the other hand, asserts: "The Nicene Creed erected the first dike against the dissolution of dogma into Greek metaphysics"; *Der Ausgang der altkirchlichen Christologie: Eine Untersuchung über Theodor von Pharan und seine Zeit als Einführung in die alte Dogmengeschichte* (Berlin, 1957), p. 21.

development of dogma—that is, to the casting of Christianity in hellenic forms."[46]

This interpretation of the development of dogma rests on a partial and distorted reading of "the intellectual effort of the early centuries" in both the Greek East and the Latin West. To put the issue of hellenization into historical context, there is also value in studying the development of Christian doctrine in a cultural and intellectual ambience that was decidedly nonhellenic—the Syriac. The description of the relation between Jesus and God in the theological tractates (or "homilies") of Aphrahat, the earliest of the Syriac church fathers, shows a christology that is orthodox according to the standards of fourth-century Christian hellenism, but that is not obliged to resort to its technical terminology.[47] And the language of Aphrahat, even in its unabashedly mythological cast, speaks with a directness to which the present-day reader may sometimes resonate more readily than he does to hellenic language.[48]

But that assumes that the language of orthodox dogma is in fact hellenic. Thus *The Future of Belief* recounts the history of the Christian idea of the Logos without referring either to its absence from the Nicene Creed (whose use of the name "light" for God has "lost its meaningfulness . . . completely") or to its roots in the *chokhmah* of the eighth chapter of the Book of Proverbs.[49] As the history not only of Logos but of all the major terms (including and especially

46. Dewart, p. 136.

47. On Aphrahat, cf. Ignacio Ortiz de Urbina, *Die Gottheit Christi bei Afrahat,* Orientalia Christiana (Rome, 1933).

48. See the concluding comments of Jean Daniélou, *The Theology of Jewish Christianity,* trans. John A. Baker (London, 1964), pp. 405–08.

49. Dewart, pp. 139–41, 214.

"light of light"[50]) demonstrates, the trinitarian and christological dogmas were as much a fundamental refutation of hellenism as they were some sort of "adaptation of hellenic concepts." Failure to observe the nuances of this history leads to the amazing historical postulate of a "hellenism in which *natura, substantia,* and *persona* were realities of common experience."[51] Such a refusal to take history seriously is "hellenic" if anything is.

The Development of Dogma

A large part of *The Future of Belief* is given over to an examination of the problem of doctrinal development. In a sense, in fact, the entire book is addressed to our theme. The author suggests "that loyalty to the Catholic Church would be best safeguarded . . . by a theory of development that would integrate contemporary experience and faith," a theory that would "account not only for the possibility of *ontogenetic* but also *phylogenetic* development."[52] Both the discovery of organic evolution and the contemporary understanding of the nature of consciousness make possible a theory of the development of dogma in which authentic change and novelty can be acknowledged—a possibility that is uniquely modern. "Of course, the idea that . . . orthodoxy *requires* the development of dogma, has not occurred to the Christian mind until recent times."[53]

Just what "recent times" means in this context becomes

50. On "light of light" in the theology of Athanasius, cf. Jaroslav Pelikan, *The Light of the World: A Basic Image in Early Christian Thought* (New York, 1962), pp. 53–72.

51. Dewart, p. 146.

52. Ibid., pp. 90, 97 (ital. in orig.).

53. Ibid., p. 150 (ital. in orig.).

explicit in a historical judgment that occurs at least twice in the course of the book. According to Dewart, it is possible to discern historically "Christianity's conscious decision, especially since the end of the eighteenth century, to avoid developing dogma as far as possible."[54] Somewhat later this decision is expanded into "a policy which Christianity unconsciously began to develop at some time between the days of patristic hellenism and the age of medieval Scholasticism, and which had been implicitly espoused since the beginning of the sixteenth century and consciously abided by since the end of the eighteenth."[55] It would seem, then, that there has been a development not only of dogma but also of resistance to the idea of development—from unconscious to implicit to conscious. Elsewhere this policy is traced to "a partly conscious, partly unconscious, commitment to a supposedly final conceptualization."[56]

To the student of the development of doctrine there is some irony in the designation of the end of the eighteenth century as the point when "Christianity"—that is to say, Roman Catholicism—consciously decided to avoid developing dogma. For 1854 (the dogma of the immaculate conception), 1870 (the dogma of papal infallibility), and 1950 (the dogma of the assumption) are the specific points at which the development of dogma was not only acknowledged de facto but promulgated de jure. It is significant in this connection that mariological doctrine, which has become the *cause célèbre* of the problem of development of dogma, especially since *Munificentissimus Deus,* is mentioned only once in Dewart's book and then in a brief foot-

54. Ibid., p. 108.
55. Ibid., p. 172.
56. Ibid., p. 135.

note.[57] An earlier *cause célèbre* of development of dogma, which played a role in relations with the East somewhat similar to that played by mariology in relations with Protestantism, is the double procession of the Holy Spirit; this, too, is disposed of in a footnote: "And, to be sure, filioque."[58] But since these developments of dogma helped to precipitate schism merely between churches rather than between the churches and "a world come of age," they appear to be irrelevant to the central thesis.

Underlying Dewart's historical judgments about development of dogma appears to be an even more basic historical judgment: "It is not until our own day that such a possibility [for Christian consciousness to create the concepts whereby to elaborate itself] has begun to emerge."[59] This helps to explain a parenthetical remark near the beginning of the book about "the contemporary world, which is the only real one."[60] The charges of "underdevelopment" and the calls for further development are based on the assumption that past developments represented an accommodation to their times—"*natura, substantia,* and *persona* were realities of common experience" in hellenism—and on the assumption that the adult world of the twentieth century demands a development of dogma that will catch up with its maturity.

But if the underlying problem is an understanding of Christian doctrine that has absolutized the past, is it really much of an improvement to absolutize the present moment instead? As there are aspects of tradition which Christians

57. Ibid., p. 199, n. 25.
58. Ibid., p. 142, n. 18.
59. Ibid., p. 136.
60. Ibid., p. 16.

today find appealing and others from which they feel alien-
ated, so previous ages in the history of the Church have
had to struggle to come to terms with the whole of Christian
truth, boggling at some of the very things that have assumed
such importance for believers today. As later chapters in
this book will seek to document, the development of Christian doctrine has not been a unilinear progress, but has
been characterized by an openness simultaneously to the
past and to the present, while heresy has attempted either
to absolutize a particular stage in the development or to
sacrifice continuity to relevance.

The Crisis of Continuity

Near the end of *The Future of Belief,* Dewart refers to
the "crisis of authority," suggesting that it "may be at bot-
tom the crisis of absolute theism"; and he contemplates
rather dispassionately "the eventual disappearance of Christianity in the form in which we have known it since primitive times."[61] From this it would seem that an even deeper
crisis is a crisis of continuity: if "the form" of Christianity
since primitive times is to disappear, all previous discontinuities—between the apocalyptic and the institutional,
between "charismatic authority" and "ecclesiastical office,"[62] between Jewish and non-Jewish observance—seem
together to constitute "the form." The book does contain
references to "the faithful continuity of the truth of
[Christian] doctrine," and to "the continuity of God's self-
communication to man, and the continuity of man's

61. Ibid., p. 204.
62. Cf. Hans Freiherr von Campenhausen, *Kirchliches Amt und geistliche
Vollmacht in den ersten drei Jahrhunderten* (Tübingen, 1953).

31

correlative religious experience in response to God's initiative."[63]

Yet when Dewart gets down to specifying what he means by continuity, the picture becomes rather different. The cool acceptance of discontinuity in church dogma is matched by the assumption that "Judaeo-Christianity is in uninterrupted temporal and cultural continuity with the history of man"; likewise, authentic faith takes place in "the continuity of achieving-belief and achieved-belief."[64] Therefore, Paul Tillich's reference to "the classical theology of all centuries" is repeated several times in a polemic against the failure of Tillich to be as radical in his reinterpretation of the doctrine of God as he was in his use of the doctrines of the Trinity and the incarnation.[65]

The historical assumption behind such discussions as these seems simultaneously to exaggerate and to underestimate the continuity in the development of Christian doctrine: to exaggerate it because, despite an oblique reference to Theodore Mopsuestia,[66] the discussions ignore the variations within patristic doctrine or, for that matter, within medieval doctrine as represented by the Victorines, Duns Scotus, and Nicholas Cusanus; to underestimate it because, despite its title, *The Future of Belief* is chiefly concerned with concepts and theories, not with beliefs and practices. Worship is referred to occasionally, as in the suggestion that someday Christians may "look back with amusement on the day when it was thought particularly appropriate that the believer should bend his knee in order

63. Dewart, pp. 109, 114.

64. Ibid., pp. 123, 65.

65. Ibid., pp. 38–40, 48, referring to Paul Tillich, *Ultimate Concern* (New York, 1965), pp. 45–46.

66. Dewart, p. 150.

to worship God."[67] There appears to be no explicit reference to prayer.

Yet worship has been the source from which some Christian doctrines have developed. Certainly one defensible definition of Christian theism would be that it is an attempt to give an account in concepts of the belief at work in the Christian practice of prayer. The practice of prayer has undoubtedly fluctuated in the history of the Church. But in the light of Dewart's rejection of "the distinction between language and thought,"[68] is there not some massive continuity in the daily repetition of the Our Father since primitive times? In Newman's favorite phrase from Augustine, "securus iudicat orbis terrarum."[69] Again, is the continuity in the celebration of the eucharist, in the administration of baptism, in the preaching, teaching, and reading of Scripture, in obedience to the gospel purely formal and external? Even on Dewart's own terms, it cannot be.

THE INTERRELATION BETWEEN HISTORY AND THEOLOGY

The questions about doctrinal development raised by Newman in 1845 and by Dewart more than a century later are, to be sure, more than historical. But they are also not less than historical. The final truth or falsity of these claims does not rest only on the validity of their historical judgments. At the same time, historical judgments do play both a diagnostic and a prescriptive role even in Dewart's cri-

67. Ibid., p. 204.
68. Ibid., p. 104.
69. Augustine, *Contra epistolam Parmeniani* iii.24, *CSEL 51*, 131. On the place of these "palmary words" in Newman's conversion, cf. the notes of Martin J. Svaglic, ed., John Henry Cardinal Newman, *Apologia pro Vita Sua: Being a History of His Religious Opinions* (Oxford, 1967), pp. 543–44.

tiques. In Newman's version of the problem of development, far more than in Dewart's, the historical premises are
decisive, even though the conclusion which Newman drew
from those premises was theological, not merely historical.

The relation between the historical and the theological
components of Newman's position on doctrinal development is not easy to determine. On the face of it, the argument of the *Essay on Development* appears to move from
historical fact to theological conclusion. The structure and
the sequence of the seven "tests" are in many ways highly
artificial, as Newman acknowledged by revising them so
considerably in the edition of 1878, where he spoke of
"notes" instead.[70] Nevertheless, he does give the impression
of looking for a theological position that will square with
the historical data as he has presented them. But even his
most ardent defender will concede that, at least in part, he
selected and arranged the historical data to suit a theological
position at which he was already in the process of arriving.
It lies beyond the scope of this book to trace the course of
Newman's own development, but it would certainly be
necessary to place the *Essay on Development* into some sort
of dialectical relation both with the *Apologia pro Vita Sua*
and with the *Grammar of Assent* before one could formulate
any hypothesis about the role that his historical study played
in his conversion. As one biographer has put it, "the theory
of development was intimately connected with his own
development."[71]

70. Cf. Charles Frederick Harrold, ed., John Henry Cardinal Newman,
An Essay on the Development of Christian Doctrine (New York, 1949), for
a detailed comparison of the editions of 1845 and 1878.

71. Meriol Trevor, *Newman: The Pillar of the Cloud, 1* (Garden City,
1962), 285.

Even if it were based upon such an analysis, moreover, this hypothesis would also have to deal with the obverse side of the question, namely, the role of Newman's conversion in his historical study. For it is no less clear that his developing theological position enabled, or compelled, him to look at his texts in a different way. The very questions he was putting to the texts were revised by his own spiritual odyssey. The contrasts he noted between the first centuries and the post-Nicene development, for example, became visible to him in the light of the inadequacies he had begun to discover in the Anglo-Catholic view of tradition and continuity. His historical research made him a different kind of theologian, indeed a different kind of Christian, from what he had been before; but his religious self-examination and his theological reflection also made him a different kind of historian. Whether it made him a better kind of historian is, to be sure, quite another matter.

Such questions about the interrelation between history and theology have proved to be inescapable for any scholar concerned with the study of doctrinal development. If, like Newman or Dewart, the scholar is primarily a theologian or a philosopher rather than a historian, he can be expected to be especially sensitive to the methodological implications of the interrelation. If, like Harnack, he is primarily a historian, he will need to be reminded that these implications are present and that they work in both directions, even when he does not recognize them.[72]

Beginning with Newman himself, however, most of the explicit attention to the question of development of doctrine has come from theologians rather than from historians, and with good reason; for if this chapter is correct in its

72. See Glick, pp. 105–11.

treatment of development of doctrine as the line of de-marcation between Protestantism and Roman Catholicism, theologians who ignore this issue are neglecting one of the most crucial chapters in dogmatics. Yet as a result of the theologians' concern, one side of the interrelation between history and theology has been emphasized at the expense of the other. With due recognition of the precision and depth which this approach has brought to the issue, there does seem to be a need for some reconsideration of the role that historical study as such can play in the controversy over doctrinal development.

2
The Role of
Historical Study

Newman began to work on the *Essay on Development* in March 1844. In the front of the notebook in which he was to set down his ideas and fragments for the *Essay,* he instructed himself: "Write it historically, not argumentatively. Begin . . . historically."[1] One of the Anglican replies to the *Essay on Development,* that of William Archer Butler, caught the importance of this factor in Newman's argument. "It is essential to this theory," wrote Butler, "to abide *all* true historical conclusions"; for Newman, he argued, history could not be "merely the narrative of facts, but the law of doctrine." Therefore, "the fundamental error of the whole system indeed may probably be stated to consist in this very thing, that it conceives Christianity is to be investigated *as a mere succession of historical events* in order to determine Faith."[2]

For that very reason, however, the most severe historical test to which Newman's theory of doctrinal development has been subjected came not from some "mere succession of historical events" but from one historical event in the development of Christian doctrine. On November 1, 1950, Pope Pius XII proclaimed it to be "a dogma divinely re-

1. Papers on *Development;* copy book and fragments on *Development:* Newman MSS. in the Oratory of St. Philip Neri, Birmingham (microfilm in the Yale University Library), B2.I and B2.II, Batch 135.
2. William Archer Butler, *Letters on Romanism in Reply to Mr. Newman's Essay on Development* (2d ed. Cambridge, 1858), p. 144 (ital. in orig.).

vealed that the immaculate Mother of God, the Ever-Virgin Mary, when the course of her earthly life was run, was assumed in body and in soul to heavenly glory."[3] Unlike some earlier definitions of dogma, the promulgation of the dogma of the assumption of the Blessed Virgin did not provoke any widespread controversy within the Roman Catholic communion about the substance of the doctrine. It had been generally believed by the people and taught by the theologians for a long time, and petitions signed by millions of the faithful had been importuning successive popes throughout this century and before to define it as binding *de fide* upon the entire Church.[4]

What the definition of the dogma did provoke was a very widespread and still continuing controversy over the method by which the doctrine of the assumption was defined and over the process by which it had developed.[5] Pope Pius did not attempt to prove that the doctrine of the assumption was taught as such in Scripture or confessed in the earliest documentary witnesses to the Christian and Catholic faith. Instead, he attached his promulgation of the dogma to the development of a tradition for which there is admittedly "no authentic witness . . . among the Fathers of either the East or the West prior to the end of

3. Apostolic Constitution *Munificentissimus Deus* in H. Denzinger ed., *Enchiridion symbolorum definitionum et declarationum de rebus fidei et morum* (32d ed., Freiburg Br., 1963), pp. 781–82.

4. Cf. W. Hentrich and R. W. de Moos, *Petitiones de Assumptione corporea B. V. Mariae in caelum definienda ad S. Sedem delatae* (2 vols. Vatican City, 1942).

5. Much of the debate about the definability of the assumption is summarized in Edward A. Wuenschel, "The Definability of the Assumption," *Proceedings of the Second Annual Meeting of the Catholic Theological Society of America* (1947), pp. 72–102.

the fifth century."[6] Even the most extravagant mariologists among the early fathers are silent, or certainly ambiguous, when they discuss how "the course of her earthly life" ended.[7] Yet as of the twentieth century it suddenly became part of the Catholic faith to teach the doctrine of the assumption, and it became heresy to deny it.

HISTORICAL THEOLOGY

What can it mean for a doctrine to "become" part of the Catholic faith, which is, by definition, universal both in space and in time, the faith of the apostles and of the evangelists, of the fathers and of the brethren? What, moreover, are the limits within which such "becoming" is legitimate? Polemical theology must debate the issues of legitimacy and limit; dogmatic theology must strive to formulate some a priori judgments about the development of doctrine. But it is up to historical theology to trace the processes of development. For the promulgation of any doctrine has an unavoidable ex post facto clause in it, as the familiar Vincentian canon of "quod ubique, quod semper, quod ab omnibus creditum est" suggests by its insistence upon continuity and universality.[8] Where the same thing does not seem to have been believed and taught "everywhere, always,

6. Lawrence P. Everett, "Mary's Death and Bodily Assumption" in Juniper P. Carol, ed., *Mariology* (3 vols. Milwaukee, 1955–61), 2, 483.

7. Walter J. Burghardt, *The Testimony of the Patristic Age Concerning Mary's Death* (Westminster, Md., 1957).

8. Vincent of Lérins, *Commonitorium primum* iii, *PL 50*, 640; he does, however, also allow for development of "profectus religionis": ibid. xxiii, *PL 50*, 667–68. The Vincentian canon did not become a matter of extensive discussion until the Reformation and even later: cf. for example, Josef

by everyone," the Church of later centuries may have to choose from among various teachings, elevating one to the status of official dogma and condemning others as heretical; so it did, to cite the most notorious instance, in the condemnation of Origenism.[9] But in *Munificentissimus Deus* a doctrine was defined not in response to the conflicts among the fathers but in reaction to their silence.

Such a definition makes acute the general problem of development of doctrine, which Karl Rahner has identified with characteristic precision and candor: "Among the doctrines of the Church there are many that are characterized by this, that in their explicit and palpable formulation they have not always been present in the Church and in its consciousness of faith." Such a doctrine "has, in some sense or other, 'developed.'" For it must be acknowledged that "in the form in which it is now presented it did not yet exist at the beginning of the proclamation of the gospel."[10]

How then does a doctrine develop, and what makes a doctrine definable? An entire library of dogmatic and polemical theology, too vast for consideration here, has arisen around these questions. It seems safe to estimate that more has been written about development of doctrine since 1950 than was written between Newman's *Essay* and

---

Rupert Geiselmann, *Die lebendige Überlieferung als Norm des christlichen Glaubens, dargestellt im Geiste der Traditionslehre Johannes Ev. Kuhns* (Freiburg, 1959), pp. 209–10, on the importance of Vincent for Kuhn's view of tradition and development.

9. Cf. E. von Ivánka, "Zur geistesgeschichtlichen Einordnung des Origenismus," *Byzantinische Zeitschrift, 44* (1951), 291–303; Cyril C. Richardson, "The Condemnation of Origen," *Church History, 6* (1937), 50–64.

10. Rahner, "Zur Frage der Dogmenentwicklung," *Schriften zur Theologie, 1,* 49.

the promulgation of the dogma of the assumption.[11] The relation between the Roman Catholic and the Protestant attitudes toward development of doctrine seems to have shifted. The polemicists of the Counter-Reformation, from Eck to Bossuet, charged the Reformers with introducing new and unheard-of doctrines; now this charge is being leveled by Protestant critics of the new dogma.[12]

All other considerations aside, it is certainly wholesome that the problem of development of doctrine has finally moved into prominence. It actually underlay many of the earlier debates over such doctrines as justification by faith and the authority of Scripture, but it was only with the rise of historicism in the eighteenth and nineteenth centuries that it could present itself for consideration in the form it has now taken. The recognition that the concept of development has itself developed brings a welcome clarity to an issue that has often been confused when it has not been overlooked. The fact of development of doctrine, therefore, is beyond dispute. As John Courtney Murray pointed out in the words quoted earlier, "Above all, the question is, what are the limits of development and growth?"[13]

Since the doctrine of the assumption of the Virgin Mary has been the occasion for the debate, the issues of legitimacy and limit are most often applied to the development of mariological doctrine.[14] While the fact of development is

11. See the summary and discussion by Hubert Hammans, *Die neueren katholischen Erklärungen der Dogmenentwicklung* (Essen, 1965), esp. pp. 113–17 and the extensive bibliography, pp. ix–xxii; also Rahner, ibid., pp. 49–50, n. 1.

12. Cf. Owen Chadwick, *From Bossuet to Newman: The Idea of Doctrinal Development* (Cambridge, 1957), esp. pp. 1–20 on Bossuet.

13. Murray, *The Problem of God*, p. 53.

14. Cf. Henri Rondet, *Do Dogmas Change?* trans. Mark Pontifex (New

undeniable and the issues of legitimacy and limit are un-avoidable, it is no less true that the process of development of doctrine has not been adequately investigated by historical theology. Indeed, the fact of development cannot be appreciated nor the issues of legitimacy and limit adjudicated until the processes of doctrinal development have been charted with greater accuracy. For this task of charting, the prominence of the mariological question in the literature on development is unfortunate. Everyone would admit that it certainly dramatizes both the fact and the issues, but no one would maintain that it typifies the processes.[15] Moreover, among the many doctrinal questions associated with the place of the Virgin Mary, the assumption is by common consent the one dogma whose development raises the most difficult problems.[16] Even the immaculate conception had a history that could be traced from early days.

The predominance of these questions in both theological and historical discussions of development of doctrine has affected not only the dogmatic theologians who have dealt with development as a problem, but also the historical theologians who have a responsibility to deal with it as a phenomenon. It is interesting that historians themselves sometimes leave their historical studies behind when they

---

York, 1961), pp. 35–41; John Courtney Murray, "Foreword" to Cyril Vollert, *A Theology of Mary* (New York, 1965), pp. 9–11, and Father Vollert's own discussion, pp. 223–50; also Bernard Lonergan, "The Assumption and Theology," *Collection* (London, 1967), pp. 68–83.

15. Charles Journet, "Scripture and the Immaculate Conception: A Problem in the Evolution of Dogma," in Edward Dennis O'Connor, ed., *The Dogma of the Immaculate Conception: History and Significance* (Notre Dame, 1958), pp. 3–48.

16. Cf. R. L. P. Milburn, *Early Christian Interpretations of History* (New York, 1954), pp. 161–92.

come to the consideration of development of doctrine. Thus Newman's *Essay* does not contain many historical nuggets that match some of the excursuses in the editions of Athanasius.[17] Rahner's essay refers repeatedly to the need for a posteriori consideration of development of doctrine in the light of concrete historical research, but his own historical research is largely excluded from his collected works.[18] Turner acknowledges "the mere fact of development" of doctrine, but then goes right on to discuss "the value or the truth of the results of the process."[19] Nevertheless, the process deserves to be studied in its own right, quite apart from the value or the truth of its results. Church historians have been challenged so often to justify themselves and their discipline on theological grounds that they, too, make undue haste to argue problems of value and truth.

The Function of Church History

The investigation of the development of Christian doctrine in the history of theology is too important to be left to the theologians. It is an occupational hazard for theolo-

17. See his note, "On the Alleged Confession of Antioch against Paul of Samosata," *Select Treatises of S. Athanasius*, A Library of Fathers of the Holy Catholic Church, 8 (Oxford, 1842), 165–76.

18. Many readers of Rahner's theological work, for example, are not aware that he has investigated much of the early history of the doctrine of penance in a series of articles: "Zur Theologie der Busse bei Tertullian: Abhandlungen über Theologie und Kirche," *Festschrift für Karl Adam,* ed. M. Reding (Düsseldorf, 1952), pp. 139–67; "Die Busslehre des hl. Cyprian von Karthago," *Zeitschrift für katholische Theologie,* 75 (1952), 252–76; "Busslehre und Busspraxis der Didascalia Apostolorum," ibid., 72 (1950), 257–81; "La doctrine d'Origène sur la pénitence," *Recherches de science religieuse, 37* (1950), 47–97, 252–86.

19. H. E. W. Turner, *The Pattern of Christian Truth* (London, 1954), pp. 487–88.

gians, even for those who have done historical work, to suppose that "to penetrate to the history of doctrine, we must eliminate from consideration what is commonly understood as the tumult of church history." The theologian who voiced that judgment had himself carried on some very impressive research into the church history of the Sinai peninsula, which was uncompleted because of his untimely death. But he also maintained that "in order to gain an insight into the dialectical process [of the history of doctrine], we must abstract from the biographical and political circumstances, that is, from the phenomena which we usually designate as church historical."[20] It is not at all clear just what function is left for church history in this definition of the scope of the history of doctrine, except perhaps to describe the scenery in front of which the essentially theological dialogue has been taking place. Yet that very dialogue has insisted all along that the relation is the other way around, that doctrine develops within the common life of the Church.[21]

At the same time, the history of the development of doctrine also deserves to be studied in its own right, without constantly being interpreted as an explicit function of the organizational, political, and liturgical life of the Church. The development of doctrine has an integrity of its own, no less than, for example, the development of polity or of liturgy or of exegesis. It was in reaction against an excessively "dialectical" handling of the materials of the history of doctrine that certain critics were led to argue that the

20. Elert, *Ausgang*, pp. 324–26.

21. See John Coulson's account of Newman's controversies with Gillow, Franzelin, and others, "Introduction" to John Henry Newman, *On Consulting the Faithful in Matters of Doctrine* (New York, 1961), pp. 1–49.

history of Christian doctrine is not a proper discipline of historical research, and that the development of doctrine in a particular time and place may be interpreted competently only by a scholar whose field of concentration is the entire culture of those centuries. Indeed, the most formidable of these specialists, Eduard Schwartz, went on to question whether there is a proper discipline even of church history, since this, too, foreshortens its research by looking for the explanation of the phenomena with which it deals outside their historical context.[22]

There are many studies of the history of doctrine that merit this condemnation by their failure to examine the subtle ties of thought and feeling between a theologian or a churchman and the *Zeitgeist*. But there may also be ties that connect him, for better or for worse or for some combination of the two, to his ancestors, sometimes to his distant ancestors, more securely than to his contemporaries or immediate predecessors. It is important to see Martin Luther in relation to the fifteenth century in which he was born; just how important it is, we are only now beginning to discover as painstaking research begins to supply the missing links.[23] But in some ways the apostles and the prophets were more his contemporaries than were any of the late medieval doctors, and many of his thoughts and doctrines were decisively shaped by Augustine rather than by Lyra or Burgensis or Cardinal Hugo, despite his many

22. Eduard Schwartz, "Über Kirchengeschichte," *Gesammelte Schriften* (Berlin, 1938 ff.), *1*, 110–30.

23. See, for example, Gerhard Ebeling, "Die Anfänge von Luthers Hermeneutik," *Zeitschrift für Theologie und Kirche, 48* (1951), 172–230; and "Luthers Auslegung des 44. (45.) Psalms," *Lutherforschung heute*, Referate and Berichte des 1. Internationalen Lutherforschungskongresses Aarhus, 18.–23. August 1956 (Berlin, 1958), pp. 32–48.

citations of them all.[24] Increasingly it becomes evident that the historian of English literature needs to read Milton not only in the context of Puritanism but also in relation to Dante and to the entire epic tradition.[25] It is no less important to see that the development of Christian doctrine, by its very nature as thought but churchly thought, is bound simultaneously to each of the particular cultural situations within which men have reflected on the Christian message and to the successions within which these men have stood.

Dogmengeschichte as Study of Church Doctrine

The historical study of the development of doctrine is largely the creation of German Protestant scholarship during the eighteenth and nineteenth centuries.[26] Despite the prolegomena with which it has usually begun, setting forth the definition of its "office" as the study of church doctrine,[27] *Dogmengeschichte* has concentrated not on the history of what the Church believed, taught, and confessed,

---

24. Cf. Ernst Schäfer, *Luther als Kirchenhistoriker* (Gütersloh, 1897); W. Köhler, *Luther und die Kirchengeschichte* (Erlangen, 1900); and the work of Headley, referred to on p. 14, n. 13 above. Unfortunately, except for the works of Johannes Ficker and a few other scholars, none of the standard editions of Luther is sufficiently documented to provide the basis for a critical study of his sources.

25. Cf. Thomas Greene, *The Descent from Heaven: A Study in Epic Continuity* (New Haven, 1963), pp. 363–418.

26. Cf. Peter C. Hodgson, *The Formation of Historical Theology: A Study of Ferdinand Christian Baur,* Makers of Modern Theology, ed. Jaroslav Pelikan (New York 1966).

27. Reinhold Seeberg, *Text-Book of the History of Doctrines,* trans. Charles E. Hay (2 vols. new printing, Grand Rapids, 1952), *1,* 19–22: "Definition and Office of the History of Doctrines."

but on the history of erudite theology. Thus it has been a specialized chapter of the general history of thought, analogous to (and, for certain periods, virtually identical with) the history of learning and of philosophy.

The history of Christian doctrine in the Middle Ages is probably the most flagrant case of such reductionism. It has been so completely dominated by the history of philosophical systems and ideas that, in the words of an eminent medievalist, "during the past hundred years the general tendency among historians of medieval thought seems to have been to imagine the Middle Ages as peopled by philosophers rather than theologians."[28] The Middle Ages were, in fact, peopled by baptized members of the Church, some of whom went on to become theologians and philosophers. How these people prayed and did penance, how they heard and obeyed the word of God, and how they expected the resurrection of the dead and the life of the age to come— these would all seem to be proper objects of the historian's curiosity and research, alongside their study of the Greek philosophers, their theories about universals, and their opinions about the demonstrability of the existence of God.

A large part of this sort of research into the development of Christian doctrine can come only from the historian rather than from the theologian. When Karl Holl finished his study of the evolution of the penitential practice within the structures of Basilian monasticism, he managed to illumine the connection between private revelation and ecclesiastical structures as has no scholar before or since.[29] Who

28. Etienne Gilson, "Historical Research and the Future of Scholasticism," *A Gilson Reader*, ed. Anton C. Pegis (Garden City, 1957), p. 156.

29. Karl Holl, *Enthusiasmus und Bussgewalt beim griechischen Mönchtum* (Leipzig, 1898).

but the specialist in early church history could have made sense of this material, or of the development of the Filioque? Similarly, Perry Miller was working as a church historian when he analyzed the connections and the contrasts between the Puritan notion of the covenant and its English and Continental counterparts; thereby he changed decisively the understanding of what Calvinism and Arminianism meant in the development of the doctrines of sin and grace in colonial America.[30]

What is more, the full range of the life of the Church within its culture must be studied if the lines of development are to be understood. Thus Turner's emphasis on the *lex orandi* as the principle of discernment within the "penumbra" of orthodoxy and heresy in the second century is a valuable corrective to the brilliant overstatements in Walter Bauer's influential monograph on the subject;[31] but, to put both orthodoxy and heresy into context, many other factors in addition to the *lex orandi* would have to be examined, as Turner himself acknowledged.[32] Only from detailed *explication de texte* that resonates to the various accents of the times can there come a responsible judgment about the various processes by which various doctrines have in fact developed in various periods. To be rescued from theological or philosophical apriorism, the study of the development of Christian doctrine needs total immersion in the concrete life of the Church's past.

30. Cf. Perry Miller, *The New England Mind,* Vol. 1: *The Seventeenth Century* (Boston, 1961), pp. 365–97, 502–05.

31. The second edition of Walter Bauer, *Rechtgläubigkeit und Ketzerei im ältesten Christentum,* ed. Georg Strecker (Tübingen, 1964), contains, on pp. 293–300, an interesting defense of Bauer by Strecker against Turner.

32. See, for example, Turner, pp. 462–63.

Change and Continuity

The historian of doctrine, like most other historians, tends to be more interested in change than in continuity. Therefore, it is the novelty of a teaching in comparison with its antecedents that becomes the focal point of his discussion, determining the headings of his chapters and the periodization of his history. This interest in change takes the form of a preoccupation with doctrinal controversy and with theological speculation, to produce the impression that the development of Christian doctrine is far more erratic and fitful than it has in fact been. A doctrine is taken up at the point where it became a matter of controversy. The several parties and speculative alternatives are ranged across the battlefield, the thrusts and counterthrusts are detailed, and the eventual victory of orthodoxy is described. Then the doctrine is scarcely heard from again until some later figure decides that it is in need of speculative reconsideration. It is of course inevitable and proper, if development of doctrine is to be the assignment, that the historian concentrate on the origins and growth of each doctrine itself; one cannot be expected to include what everyone has thought about everything.

Yet that does not necessarily imply that one must concentrate on doctrinal controversy and on theological speculation for their own sakes, rather than as eruptions of church doctrine; this would be to assume that all doctrines always originate within controversy and that they usually grow and develop as a result of speculation. Some doctrines do originate in controversy and some grow through speculation, but others certainly originate and grow within the Church in other ways. To cite one instance, according to

Newman "the Real Presence appears by the Liturgies of the fourth or fifth century to have been the doctrine of the earlier."[33] Hence it is not good history to reserve discussion of eucharistic theology until one comes to the debate between Ratramnus and Radbertus during the ninth century in the West, simply because there seems to have been relatively little speculation and even less controversy about the real presence before that time.[34] Nor does it seem historically sound to publish in its entirety the treatise of Ratramnus, which may in some ways be regarded as an ancestor of Protestant eucharistic theories, but to publish only selections from the treatise of Radbertus, which came closer to the Catholic consensus.[35] For similar reasons, it cannot be called a fair reading of the development of Augustine's doctrine of the Trinity when one looks only for the anticipations of its notion of trinitarian analogies and not for the sources of its trinitarian interpretation of Scripture. Yet a recent monograph on the subject dismisses the influence of Hilary of Poitiers upon Augustinian trinitarianism with the remark that "in fact, Hilary's influence does not go very deep and disappears especially at the point where Augustine goes beyond the mere proof of the dogma from Scripture."[36] It should perhaps be pointed out that

33. Newman, *Essay*, p. 23.

34. On some of the problems created by the absence of speculation and controversy about the eucharist in the early centuries, see, for example, the discussion of Irenaeus in Jesus Solano, *Textos eucaristicos primitivos* (2 vols. Madrid, 1962–64), *1*, 67–73, and 76, n. 51.

35. "For this series our interest in the work [of Radbertus] resides primarily in the fact that Ratramnus . . . presents a different view." George E. McCracken and Allen Cabaniss, eds., *Early Medieval Theology*, The Library of Christian Classics (Philadelphia, 1957), p. 92.

36. Alfred Schindler, *Wort und Analogie in Augustins Trinitätslehre* (Tübingen, 1965), p. 129.

this monograph appeared in a series entitled "Studies on Hermeneutics."

Such a way of putting the problem of development of doctrine (not to say the problem of hermeneutics) makes the continuity of Christian doctrine in the history of the Church both before and after the Protestant Reformation a source of annoyance, as it was, for example, to Harnack. At the beginning of his history Harnack speaks condescendingly of "the tenacity of ancient dogma";[37] and at the end of that history the theology of Luther is described as "the shattering of dogma,"[38] despite Luther's explicit trinitarianism and almost Alexandrian christology. But if continuity is dismissed as tenacity, the true nature of the development of doctrine is inevitably distorted. For even in violent controversy and even in audacious speculation, doctrine develops out of earlier doctrine within the context of the total life of the Church in the world. And it does not do so on the basis of the a priori logic prescribed by the theologian, but on the basis of an a posteriori logic to be described by the historian. Dramatic breaks and radical discontinuities are not all that is interesting about the process of development.

History Beyond Polemics

When the processes of development, rather than its legitimacy and its limits, become the object of historical research, the problem of development of doctrine can be lifted, at least temporarily, beyond the arena of polemical theology. While the parting of the ways between Christian

37. Adolf von Harnack, *Lehrbuch der Dogmengeschichte* (5th ed. Tübingen, 1931), *1*, 21–22.
38. Ibid., *3*, 861–63.

communities, in Father Murray's phrase, may indeed take place on the issue of development of doctrine, the historians of the several communities ought to be able to collaborate on an investigation of the processes of development. For an entire generation, philosophers and theologians have dealt with the role of presuppositions in the work of the historian and have taught historians to be exceedingly modest about claiming "scientific objectivity." This was a lesson that all historians, and particularly church historians, had to learn. But they have learned it all too well; for what has come to be disparaged as "pseudo-history" or as "philological history"[39] is, in fact, the very kind of history on which scholarship depends for a study of the processes of the development of doctrine.

Such "philological history," moreover, is a form of historical research that can transcend, though not automatically, differences among theologians of various confessional presuppositions. Thus scholars of various confessions should find it possible, by means of philological history, to trace some of the processes by which various Christian doctrines have developed in various periods. Does the development of the doctrine of the Trinity, whose results most Protestants accept, correspond to that conception of the authority of Scripture which these same Protestants maintain? Did not the Arians, rather than the orthodox, "confine themselves to the language of Scripture"?[40] On the other hand, if the definition of papal infallibility set down a century ago is retroactive, does a study of the documents bear out the contention that doctrine has in fact developed under the

39. R. G. Collingwood, *The Idea of History* (New York, 1956), pp. 299–300.
40. John Henry Newman, *The Arians of the Fourth Century* (1st ed. London, 1833), p. 237.

tutelage of an ecclesiastical magisterium so defined? If Peter spoke through the mouth of Leo at Chalcedon, as the council fathers affirmed,[41] how is the historian to deal with the circumstance that "except for the one case under Leo the Great, the West did not come into view as a partner in the discussion" of the ecumenical councils?[42]

Again, does the historical scholar have a warrant in some "patristic consent"[43] for going beyond the philologically ascertainable *ipsissima verba* of his documents and for finding in them early hints and traces of what, by subsequent development of doctrine, has become the faith of the Church Catholic? If he has such a warrant, what are its methodological limits? If he does not have it, does this require a redefinition of the processes of development? The tough questions in the development of Christian doctrine will not finally be settled by any historical research, but they can be faced theologically only when such research has done its job. And for the development of doctrine, that job is primarily one of investigating the history of the early Church, as Newman recognized.

THE TASK OF PATRISTIC RESEARCH

Despite his astonishingly wide, if rather desultory, reading both in primary sources and in secondary accounts,

41. Cf. Hugo Rahner, "Leo der Grosse, der Papst des Konzils" in Aloys Grillmeier and Heinrich Bacht, eds., *Das Konzil von Chalkedon: Geschichte und Gegenwart, 1* (Würzburg, 1959), 323–39.

42. Bernhard Kötting, "Die abendländischen Teilnehmer an den ersten allgemeinen Konzilen" in Erwin Iserloh and Konrad Repgen, eds., *Reformata Reformanda: Festgabe für Hubert Jedin zum 17. Juni 1965, 1* (Münster Westf., 1965), 21.

43. Walter J. Burghardt, "Mary in Western Patristic Thought" in Carol, *Mariology, 1,* 109–10.

Newman relied in the *Essay* on authorities who "apart from Guizot and Gieseler . . . are patristic authorities. He was not reading Möhler, nor Wiseman, nor Perrone, nor even Petau. He was reading Justin Martyr, Athanasius, Tertullian, Ambrose, Lactantius, Cyril."[44] Chapters IV and V of the *Essay,* which are an application of the first test, "Preservation of Type or Idea," to the data of church history, deal seriatim with the first three centuries, with the fourth century, and with the fifth and sixth centuries.[45] Later sections relate some of the other tests to medieval and modern history as well, but the principal historical substance is derived from Newman's patristic research.

The reason for this is not only that Newman happened to be primarily a patristic scholar. It is also that the problem of development of doctrine must be dealt with on the basis of the church fathers, or it is not being dealt with at all. As we have seen, Harnack was in many ways Newman's polar antithesis as an interpreter of the development of doctrine. Nevertheless, they were one in the insistence that "the center of gravity of church history as a scholarly field lies in the history of the Church and of dogma during the first six centuries."[46] Thus if the problem of doctrinal development is basic to the ecumenical discussion and if the problem requires historical study, an indispensable part of true ecumenical responsibility must be a more fundamental study of patristic literature and thought. Although we cannot study ourselves into reconciliation, it is equally true

44. Chadwick, *From Bossuet to Newman,* p. 119; cf. also D. Gorce, *Newman et les pères* (Paris, 1934).

45. Newman, *Essay,* pp. 203–17.

46. Adolf von Harnack, "Denkschrift vom 27. September 1888," quoted in Agnes von Zahn-Harnack, *Adolf von Harnack,* p. 129.

that any reconciliation that ignores or bypasses the church fathers will be more shallow and superficial for this neglect. To an extent that polemical theologians on both sides have not recognized, the methods of careful historical and philological scholarship can transcend the dogmatic (or anti-dogmatic) presuppositions of the scholar and can thus lead to results that go beyond polemics to truth and thus, hopefully, a little closer to unity.

Philological Research in the Fathers

It is not surprising that the theology of the church fathers claims a place in current efforts at Christian understanding, for it has had a prominent place in the sorry history of Christian misunderstanding. The East and the West were separated by their ignorance of each other's fathers long before they were divided by formal schism and mutual excommunication.[47] The "critical reverence" of Luther and his colleagues toward patristic tradition was an important issue in the debates of the Reformation.[48] It is becoming clear both how little Luther knew of Thomas Aquinas and how little some Thomists have known of the church fathers.[49] But even from these instances it would be naïve to suppose that historical research in the study of the fathers is never anything more than the effort to prove the rightness of one's confessional stance or of one's personal position.

47. Berthold Altaner, "Augustinus in der griechischen Kirche bis auf Photius," *Kleine patristische Schriften,* ed. Günter Glockmann (Berlin, 1967), pp. 57–98.

48. Pelikan, *Obedient Rebels,* pp. 25–104.

49. Cf. Otto Hermann Pesch, *Theologie der Rechtfertigung bei Martin Luther und Thomas von Aquin* (Mainz, 1967), esp. pp. 949–56; and Martin Grabmann, *Die Geschichte der scholastischen Methode* (new printing, Graz, 1957), *1,* 22, n. 2.

Although there has been plenty of such historical research, the relation can move in the opposite direction as well; the results of such research can compel reformulations or even modifications of earlier positions. A brief reference to two celebrated instances from the history of philological research in the fathers during the past one hundred years will illustrate some of the subtle interrelations between denominational loyalty and historical-literary investigation.

The first is the question of the authenticity of the traditional version of the seven epistles of Ignatius of Antioch. In the first edition of Newman's *Essay* these epistles were the chief proof for the development of "theological science" during the period immediately after the apostles.[50] The epistles have been transmitted in three divergent manuscript traditions.[51] The generally accepted text or "middle recension"[52] of the seven epistles is represented in such witnesses as the so-called Medici manuscript in Florence, although this important manuscript happens to contain only six of the seven epistles in Greek. The "long recension," present in both Greek and Latin manuscripts, is an extremely expanded version of the seven epistles, with several epistles added.[53] There is also a recension much

50. Newman, *Essay,* pp. 390–96.
51. Cf. Milton Perry Brown, *The Authentic Writings of Ignatius: A Study of Linguistic Criteria* (Durham, N. C., 1963).
52. I have adopted here the suggestion that what used to be called the "short recension" now be termed the "middle recension," in view of Cureton's edition of the Syriac texts (see n. 54 below).
53. This owed part of its authority to its publication by Faber Stapulensis in 1498. I have consulted the edition of Symphorianus Champerius, *Epistolae sanctissimorum sequenti codice contentae* (Paris, 1516), which, together with several of the books cited in the following notes, is in the Beinecke Library at Yale.

shorter than the first, available in a Syriac translation.[54]

It has been agreed since Ussher that many of the other epistles circulating under the name of Ignatius during the Middle Ages were not authentic.[55] But there has been no such agreement on the authenticity of the received text of the seven epistles of Ignatius. Because this text showed such an advanced state of doctrinal development in its emphasis on the hierarchical nature of the Church and made such explicit reference to the authority of the bishop, certain Protestant scholars insisted that this version could not have been written by Ignatius, who died during or shortly after the first decade of the second century, perhaps as early as 107.[56] Most Roman Catholic scholars, on the other hand, "maintained the authenticity and integrity of the twelve epistles of the Long Recension."[57] Each side began with a set of presuppositions and decided the question of authenticity in a way that was consistent with these.

But it was not quite that simple. For while the polemical historians were exchanging theses, antitheses, and hypotheses, other historians were patiently at work sorting out the documentary evidence and drawing reasonable conclusions from it. John Pearson, an Anglican scholar, published in 1672 a careful defense of the authenticity of all seven

54. William Cureton, *The Antient Syriac Version of the Epistles of Saint Ignatius* (London, 1845).

55. James Ussher, ed., *Appendix Ignatiana* (London, 1647), also in the Beinecke Library.

56. Thus, for example, the words *tēn phainomenēn neōterikēn taxin* in Ignatius, *Magnesians* iii, are translated by Lightfoot (see n. 57) as "his youthful state or condition," but are interpreted by Zahn (see n. 62) as referring to "the ordination of a young man." Cf. Daniel Völker, *Die ignatianischen Briefe auf ihren Ursprung untersucht* (Tübingen, 1892), p. 16, n. 1.

57. J. B. Lightfoot, ed., *The Apostolic Fathers* (2d ed. London, 1889), *1*, Pt. II, 238.

epistles, which had been attacked by the French Calvinist, Jean Daillé.[58] In 1845, the same year as Newman's *Essay,* the conflict over the Ignatian epistles erupted again, as a result of the discovery and publication by the Anglican scholar, William Cureton, of the Syriac version of three epistles of Ignatius—those to Polycarp, to the Ephesians, and to the Romans—which were the only epistles he was willing to acknowledge as authentic.[59] Once more, other Protestants joined the campaign against the traditional version of the epistles while Roman Catholics defended it, both sides on confessional grounds;[60] and Newman was moved to write his provocative epigram: "The interpolated Epistles . . . are too Scriptural to be Apostolic."[61]

Again it was Protestant historical scholarship that vindicated the authenticity of the seven epistles. Theodor Zahn, an orthodox Lutheran, published his defense in 1873.[62] And from 1885 to 1889, Joseph B. Lightfoot, by then the Anglican bishop of Durham, wrote the definitive analysis of the evidence, together with a detailed history of the research into it. The highly developed hierarchical conceptions of the bishop of Antioch were not at all congenial to

58. Jean Daillé, *De scriptis, quae sub Dionysii Areopagitae et Ignatii Antiocheni nominibus circumferuntur* . . . (Geneva, 1666), also in the Yale collection; John Pearson, *Vindiciae epistolarum S. Ignatii,* Library of Anglo-Catholic Theology (new ed. 2 vols. Oxford, 1852).

59. Cureton, pp. xvi–xxvii; also Cureton, *Corpus Ignatianum* (London, 1849), containing both those epistles which he regarded as genuine and those which he regarded as spurious.

60. Cf. John Henry Newman, "On the Text of the Seven Epistles of St. Ignatius," *Tracts, Theological and Ecclesiastical* (London, 1874), pp. 95–123; and Franz Xaver von Funk, *Die Echtheit der ignatianischen Briefe aufs neue vertheidigt* (Tübingen, 1883).

61. Newman, *Essay* (Harrold ed.), p. 109.

62. Theodor Zahn, *Ignatius von Antiochien* (Gotha, 1873).

Zahn, nor even to Bishop Lightfoot, just as, for that matter, the omission of references to the primacy of the bishop of Rome in the epistles of Ignatius was a puzzle to his Roman Catholic interpreters. But both Zahn and Lightfoot developed their literary, textual, and historical analysis with such careful attention to methodology and such sound scholarship that there is now virtually unanimous acceptance of the seven epistles in their middle recension.[63] The dispute was not settled by a priori theories about doctrinal development on either side, but by philological history and honest historical research into the facts of the development.

The conflict over Ignatius was resolved by the research of Anglicans and Lutherans, but that concerned with Cyprian was settled through the work of two Roman Catholic scholars, Maurice Bévenot and Othmar Perler. Working independently of each other, they ended the long-standing controversy over the two versions of *On the Unity of the Catholic Church*.[64] One recension is far more explicit than the other in claiming the primacy of Peter and "hanc Petri unitatem" as constitutive of the oneness of the Church as such. Naturally, the textual problem of this chapter became an issue between Roman Catholic and Protestant scholars. Wilhelm August von Hartel, who prepared the critical edi-

---

63. On the controversy since Lightfoot's time, cf. Virginia Corwin, *St. Ignatius and Christianity in Antioch* (New Haven, 1960), pp. 7–10.

64. The alternative texts are discussed and the principal alternatives evaluated in D. van den Eynde, "La double édition du De unitate de S. Cyprien," *Revue d'histoire ecclésiastique, 29* (1933), 5–24; O. Perler, "De catholicae ecclesiae unitate cap. 4–5. Die ursprünglichen Texte, ihre Überlieferung, ihre Datierung," *Römische Quartalschrift, 44* (1936), 151–68; and Maurice Bévenot, *The Tradition of the Manuscripts: A Study in the Transmission of St. Cyprian's Treatises* (Oxford, 1961), which gives a detailed presentation of the textual and philological evidence.

tion of the writings of Cyprian, contended that the passages emphasizing the primacy of Peter are a later interpolation.[65] He was joined in this contention by other Protestant scholars, including E. Watson and Hugo Koch.[66] In an answer to Hartel and Koch, J. Chapman, a convert to Roman Catholicism, suggested that both versions came from Cyprian, and that the recension stressing primacy was issued later as a further development and clarification of the other version; thus in asserting the primacy of Peter, Cyprian developed beyond his earlier formulation, in which the more general authority of all the bishops had been asserted on the basis of the office not only of Peter but of all the apostles.[67]

And there the matter stood, with Protestants contending for the correctness of what may be called the "episcopacy text" and Roman Catholics contending that the final stage of Cyprian's development was better expressed in what may be called the "primacy text." Then, during the 1930s, a significantly different conclusion was proposed: that the primacy text was the earlier one, and that the final intention of the author is represented more accurately by that reading which stresses the primacy of Peter less. On the basis of meticulous attention to the manuscript evidence and to the vocabulary and syntax of Cyprian's Latinity, this conclusion was established by Bévenot in a dissertation first published in 1937. Bévenot's edition and translation of the treatise, published twenty years after his original monograph, sum-

65. W. Hartel in *CSEL 3*, Pt. I, 213.

66. Koch, *Cyprianische Untersuchungen* (Bonn, 1926), pp. 83–131; E. Watson, "The Interpolations in Cyprian's De unitate ecclesiae," *Journal of Theological Studies, 5* (1904), 432–36.

67. J. Chapman, "Les interpolations dans la traité de S. Cyprien sur l'Unité de l'Église," *Revue bénédictine, 19* (1902), 246–54.

marizes his research admirably in its introduction: "The view here taken is that Cyprian himself revised his text, and that what is known as the 'Primacy Text' . . . is the original one, whereas the generally received text is his correction of it." Regarding the "episcopacy text" Bévenot comments: "If he altered the text of chapter four . . . this will have been *not* because he had changed his mind about the Papacy, but because Rome was reading more into it than he had intended."[68]

As Bévenot himself observes, "in more recent times, controversy has mostly been replaced by discussion, and the protagonists are no longer divided on strictly denominational lines."[69] Thus the most vigorous reassertion of the charge that the "primacy text" is a pro-Roman forgery has come from a Roman Catholic scholar, the Benedictine, J. Le Moyne.[70] On the basis of historical scholarship, then, Roman Catholics no longer feel obliged to contend for anachronisms in the history of the development of the idea of primacy; they can face the facts of that development candidly.

DOCTRINAL ISSUES AND PATRISTIC SCHOLARSHIP

For Protestant scholars to have shown the authenticity of the hierarchical epistles of Ignatius and for Roman Catholic scholars to have concluded that Cyprian "corrected" the primacy text of his treatise would appear to be a victory for

68. Maurice Bévenot, ed. and trans., "Introduction" to *Cyprian: The Lapsed; The Unity of the Catholic Church,* Ancient Christian Writers (Westminster, Md., 1957), pp. 6–7.

69. Ibid., p. 6.

70. J. Le Moyne, "Saint Cyprien est-il bien l'auteur de la rédaction brève du 'De Unitate' chapitre 4?" *Revue bénédictine, 63* (1953), 70–115.

scholarship over polemics. It does not bring about any agreement on questions of hierarchy or primacy, but it does help to preserve honesty in the disagreement. This, in turn, arouses the hope that similar study can be of use in the discussion of other issues in the problem of doctrinal development, at least some of which seem susceptible of clarification through patristic study.

The De-Judaization of Christianity

One such issue must certainly be the relation between the development of Christian doctrine and its Jewish background. The most accurate term for the treatises written *adversus Judaeos* during the first five centuries is not "hellenization" but "de-Judaization."[71] How and why did Christian thinkers become so tone-deaf to many of the religious accents of the Hebrew tradition? Jean Daniélou's explorations of the Christian interpretation of the story of the Exodus shows how fruitful a source that story was for Christian mysticism, typology, and interpretation of history.[72] Marrou even speaks of a "metaphysic of the Exodus."[73] But it is also evident that only centuries later, if ever, did some of the central themes of Jewish theology become motifs for Christian thought.[74] The loss of vital

71. Gregory Dix, *Jew and Greek: A Study in the Primitive Church* (New York, 1953), p. 109.

72. Jean Daniélou, *From Shadows to Reality: Studies in the Biblical Typology of the Fathers,* trans. Wulstan Hibberd (Westminster, Md., 1960), pp. 153–226.

73. Henri-Irénée Marrou, ed., *Clément d'Alexandrie, Le Pédagogue, 1* Sources chrétiennes, *70* (Paris, 1960), 236–37, n. 4, referring to Ex. 3:14.

74. Cf. Robert L. Wilken, "Judaism in Roman and Christian Society," *The Journal of Religion, 47* (October 1967), 313–30.

contact with Jewish exegesis of Scripture prevented Christian scholars from recognizing the biblical and rabbinical backgrounds of phrases and allusions in their own New Testament.[75]

A good beginning for historical reconsideration of relations between Judaism and Christianity would be not only a study of the treatises *adversus Judaeos* but also a new study of the condemnation of Marcion.[76] Superficially, that condemnation certainly was a justification of a bipartite Scripture consisting of both Old and New Testament as the Christian Bible. But the price that was paid for this achievement was a weakening of the Christian hold on the literal, historical sense of the Old Testament. Newman may have been right when he generalized in the *Essay on Development* that

> the Jews clung to the literal sense of the Old Testament and rejected the Gospel; the Christian Apologists proved its divinity by means of the allegorical. . . . It may be almost laid down as an historical fact, that the mystical interpretation and orthodoxy will stand or fall together.[77]

Yet in spite of the riches contributed to Christian devotion and theology by the allegorical interpretation of the Old Testament, something quite basic was lost when the his-

75. Marcel Simon, *Verus Israel: Étude sur les relations entre Chretiens et Juifs dans l'empire romain, I* (Paris, 1948), 233–38.

76. The interpretation of the controversy over Marcion continues to be dominated by Adolf von Harnack, *Marcion: Das Evangelium vom fremden Gott* (new printing Leipzig, 1960), even though recent discoveries make Harnack's definition of Gnosticism, and therefore his view of Marcion's relation to Gnosticism, obsolete; see Robert M. Grant, *Gnosticism and Early Christianity* (New York, 1959), pp. 121–28.

77. Newman, *Essay*, p. 324.

torical sense was depreciated as much as it was by the controversy with Marcion. A brand-new investigation of that controversy, in the light of what is now known about Gnosticism, could also shed light on the alienation between Judaism and Christianity.

The Definition of Unity

A second doctrinal issue that would benefit from patristic research is the definition of the unity of the Church and a careful examination of the so-called "undivided Church" of the early centuries. Newman's *Essay* is by no means the only illustration of a romanticism on all sides about the unity of the ancient Church, with many interpreters professing to find there the very same guarantees of unity to which they now point as means for the reunion of Christendom.[78] A generation ago the prevailing tendency of historical theology and of New Testament study was to emphasize the variety within the New Testament, the heterogeneity of the second and third centuries, and the discontinuity in the development between the New Testament and the early fathers. This emphasis upon discontinuity still appears among some historians, but the unity of the New Testament is more in evidence today than is its variety.[79]

Both these tendencies sidestep major difficulties in the history of doctrinal development, one of the most vexing of which is the question of continuity. There appears to be greater continuity between some parts of the New Testa-

78. Cf. Olof Linton, *Das Problem der Urkirche in der neueren Forschung* (Uppsala, 1932), for a competent summary; also John Knox, *The Early Church and the Coming Great Church* (New York, 1955).

79. This trend is well stated in C. H. Dodd, *The Apostolic Preaching and its Developments* (2d ed. New York, 1954).

ment and some parts of second-century thought than there is between those same parts of the New Testament and other parts of the New Testament. To condemn the doctrine of grace in the apostolic fathers, for example, for not being sufficiently Pauline greatly oversimplifies the development both within the first century and between it and the second.[80] There is a continuity in the doctrinal development from one century to the next, and there is a unity within any particular century; neither the continuity nor the unity can be identified with uniformity.

What is more, the variety within the total life and thought of the Church at any one time must have been considerably greater than the surviving documents show. On the doctrine of the person of Christ, for example, there are enough hints in the documents to suggest quite strongly that during the second and third centuries something akin to an "adoptionistic" explanation of the divine sonship of Christ must have had some currency among orthodox Christians, perhaps especially among those of Jewish background.[81] Eventually, adoptionism and other heresies were condemned, and properly so; but this theological judgment does not provide a historical explanation of the forces that held the early Church together in spite of an astonishing theological diversity, an organizational decentralization, and the absence of fixed norms of worship and observance.

80. Thomas F. Torrance, *The Doctrine of Grace in the Apostolic Fathers* (Edinburgh, 1948), pp. 133–41.

81. Harnack, *Lehrbuch der Dogmengeschichte, 1*, 210–25; even though much of Harnack's interpretation of various documents is questionable, his presentation did compel even conservative scholars to reckon with the "adoptionism" implicit in such passages as Acts 2:26 and the textual variants of Luke 3:22.

Historical study may help make it possible to define unity in a manner that is both sophisticated and candid.

After Cyprian, the most significant discussion of the nature of the unity of the Church was occasioned by Augustine's controversy with the Donatists, in which Cyprian's own doctrine was one of the chief issues.[82] Attacking the Donatist claim that the unity of the Church had been nullified by the sins of some of the bishops and that therefore unity was dependent on holiness, Augustine argued that the relation between unity and holiness was quite the opposite. Holiness in the Church was dependent on the unity of the Church, and the most grievous sin in this regard was schism. Where unity was preserved, the achievement of personal holiness was a developmental process rather than an accomplished fact. But does not the theological definition of empirical unity have to undergo a development similar to that which empirical holiness underwent in Augustine's thought, namely, that in some sense such unity, too, is a process and a goal rather than a prior fact? Both the unity of the Church and its holiness would then be seen as perfect gifts to the Church, but at the same time as goals for the Church's life and growth. Patristic theology seems to have been more successful in formulating the concept of growth toward holiness than in clarifying how there could also be a growth toward unity.

"Underdeveloped" Doctrines

These observations and recommendations about the role of patristic study in the discussion of doctrinal development

82. Cf. Geoffrey Grimshaw Willis, *Saint Augustine and the Donatist Controversy* (London, 1950), pp. 120–27. I have expanded the argument of this

would not be complete without at least a few comments about theological issues that are, as Leslie Dewart has termed them, "underdeveloped," having been left only partly developed by the church fathers as well as by subsequent centuries, and that therefore require clarification. It is a disservice to the patristic tradition to cultivate theological archaism as a substitute for rigor. For this reason Thomas Aquinas felt obliged to criticize and correct Augustine, gently but rigorously.[83] It may serve as a foil for our examination of the development of several doctrines in patristic theology if we give at least a glance to one or two doctrinal issues that were left unfinished by the very church fathers with whom we shall be dealing.

Christology is probably the most obvious example of doctrinal underdevelopment. The history of theology seems to justify the thesis that the dogma of the humanity of Jesus Christ has not been developed as fully as has the doctrine of his divinity. Several investigations have established, for example, that the content of the humanity of Christ was sufficiently unclear in the theology of Athanasius to make necessary the amplification supplied by the dogmatic decree of the Council of Chalcedon.[84] But even that decree was—certainly from the view of both the Greek East and especially the Syriac East[85]—an agreement to disagree rather than

paragraph in *The Finality of Jesus Christ in An Age of Universal History: A Dilemma of the Third Century* (London, 1965), pp. 31–37.

83. Étienne Gilson, "Pourquoi saint Thomas a critiqué saint Augustin?" *Archives d'histoire doctrinale et littéraire du moyen âge, I* (1926/27), 5–127.

84. Cf. pp. 106–07.

85. Cf. Paul Mouterde, "Le Concile de Chalcédoine d'après les historiens monophysites de langue syriaque," in Grillmeier and Bacht, *Das Konzil von Chalkedon, I,* 581–602.

a satisfactory development of the basic doctrine. After Chalcedon it remains true that the function of the human nature of Christ in most orthodox theology was to enable him to suffer and die, but that everything noble, imaginative, or profound in his person tended to be ascribed to his divine nature. There have been efforts to define the word "nature" in less static and more historical ways,[86] or to argue that while the dogma preserved the deposit of the faith against heresy, it has been the function of the liturgy, of biblical exegesis, and of piety to round out a fully developed picture of Jesus Christ as man.[87] All of this may be true, but it does not alter the unavoidable conclusion that the orthodox christology of two natures in one person is an underdeveloped doctrine.

Even more obviously in need of further development is the doctrine of the Holy Spirit. Historically, the doctrine of the personhood and coequality of the Holy Spirit was raised and solved in a remarkably short time. The controversy erupted about 360, with the emergence of the Pneumatomachoi, and it was settled by the Council of Constantinople in 381, when the doctrine of the Trinity reached its dogmatic formulation.[88] But the terminology in which the doctrine of the third person of the Trinity was formulated was a terminology mined and minted during the controversies over the second person of the Trinity. The terms *persona*, *prosōpon*, and *hypostasis*, as well as such terms as *perichōrēsis*, came out of the debates about

86. Rahner, "Probleme der Christologie von heute," *Schriften zur Theologie, 1*, 169–222.

87. Cf. Elert, *Ausgang*, pp. 12–25.

88. See Benoit Pruche, "Introduction" to Basile de Césarée, *Traité du Saint-Esprit*, Sources chrétiennes, *47* (Paris, 1946), 1–94.

the relation between the Father and the Son, to be applied now to the relation of the Spirit to the Father and the Son.[89] One element in later controversy between the Latins and the Greeks about the procession of the Holy Spirit was a lack of clarity and precision caused by the application to the Holy Spirit of terms and concepts that did not quite fit.

Yet as soon as it has been said that such doctrines as these are underdeveloped and that they need to move beyond their patristic formulations, all the questions of authenticity in doctrinal development have been raised. And these questions, in turn, push the investigation back to the history of how doctrines have in fact developed in patristic theology. Only when that history has been specified in at least some detail can the questions both of the legitimacy and of the incompleteness of past developments be dealt with by a scholarship that is informed and responsible.

89. Cf. G. L. Prestige, *God in Patristic Thought* (London, 1956), pp. 291–94, on the christological origins of *perichōrēsis*.

Part Two

Doctrinal Development
in Patristic Theology

3
Cyprian on Original Sin

One of the most striking instances of the development of Christian doctrine is the Augustinian doctrine of original sin. As Newman observed in the revised edition of the *Essay on Development,* "the recognition of Original Sin, considered as the consequence of Adam's fall, was, both as regards general acceptance and accurate understanding, a gradual process, not completed till the time of Augustine and Pelagius." In explanation of the lateness of its development, he cited the thesis, widely held by historians of doctrine today, "that the fatalism, so prevalent in various shapes pagan and heretical, in the first centuries, was an obstacle to an accurate apprehension of the consequences of the fall." Original sin, then, was "a doctrine held back for a time by circumstances, yet in the event forcing its way into its normal shape, and at length authoritatively fixed in it." It had gone through the stages of being "held implicitly, then asserting itself, and at length [being] fully developed."[1]

This analysis of the development of the doctrine of original sin is part of the conventional wisdom of textbooks on theology and the history of doctrine.[2] As it stands, however, it does not take account of the differences between the development of the doctrine of sin in Eastern, Greek Chris-

1. Newman, *Essay* (Harrold ed.), p. 117.
2. Julius Gross, *Geschichte des Erbsündendogmas: Ein Beitrag zur Geschichte des Problems vom Ursprung des Übels, 1* (Munich, 1960), 69–255; on Cyprian, cf. pp. 121–23.

tianity and that in Western, Latin Christianity, differences which Newman called attention to elsewhere.[3] Officially, to be sure, Pelagianism was a heresy in almost everyone's book.[4] Thus Thomas Aquinas, quoting Augustine, stated that "it belongs to the heresy of the Pelagians that they believe that without grace a man can keep all the divine commandments";[5] the Augsburg Confession condemned "the Pelagians and others," meaning by "the others" some of its Roman Catholic opponents;[6] even Jacob Arminius expressly disavowed any affinity with Pelagianism.[7]

The most explicit statement about Pelagius made by a synod of any church in the East appears to have been that of the synod of Diospolis or Lydda in Palestine in 415.[8] The fathers of the synod declared:

> Now since we have received satisfaction on the charges against the monk Pelagius, here present; since, too, he assents to the pious doctrines and also condemns and anathematizes what is contrary to the faith of the Church, we acknowledge that he belongs to the communion of the Catholic Church.[9]

3. Newman, *Essay* (Harrold ed.), p. 21.

4. See the discussion of recent views in Robert F. Evans, *Pelagius: Inquiries and Reappraisals* (New York, 1968), pp. 66 ff.

5. Thomas Aquinas, *Summa Theologica*, I–II, Q. 109, Art. 4, *Sancti Thomae Aquinatis . . . Opera Omnia* (new printing, New York, 1948 ff.), 2, 431.

6. Augsburg Confession, II, *The Book of Concord,* trans. Theodore G. Tappert, Jaroslav Pelikan, Robert H. Fischer, and Arthur Carl Piepkorn (Philadelphia, 1959), p. 29.

7. See G. J. Hoenderdaal, ed., *Verklaring van Jacobus Arminius* (Lochem, 1960), pp. 26–27.

8. Cf. Charles Joseph Hefele, *Histoire des conciles,* trans. Henri Leclercq (Paris, 1908), 2, Pt. I, 179, n. 1.

9. Augustine, *De gestis Pelagii* xx.44, *CSEL 42,* 99.

"The Pelagians and Caelestians" were condemned en passant at the Council of Ephesus in 431,[10] and therefore it is technically correct to say that Pelagianism is recognized as a heresy by both East and West. Hence it is probably an exaggeration for Harnack to say that "Pelagianism brought upon itself a sort of ecumenical anathema, while there were perhaps not even a dozen Christians in the East who really disapproved of it."[11] Nevertheless, the doctrine of original sin has undergone a far different development in Eastern Christendom from that which has taken place in the Western part of the Church.

AUGUSTINE ON CYPRIAN

The Western development reached its climax in the Pelagian controversy and in Augustine's formulation of the doctrine, which, with various refinements, has been acknowledged as orthodox by most of the Western Church ever since. Instead of expounding the Augustinian formulation, however, this chapter will examine one of its acknowledged antecedents in the Western development of the doctrine, as seen in the writings of Cyprian of Carthage, with a view toward identifying, if possible, some of the ways the doctrine of original sin developed from earlier stages of Christian teaching, reflection, and practice. As we have noted earlier,[12] the writings of Cyprian have been a battleground between various theories about the development of the doctrine of the unity of the Church. A battle of a differ-

---

10. Cf. Hefele-Leclercq, 2, Pt. I, 330; also Henry Chadwick, "Eucharist and Christology in the Nestorian Controversy," *The Journal of Theological Studies* (New Series), 2 (1951), 149–50.

11. Harnack, *Lehrbuch der Dogmengeschichte, 3,* 187.

12. See pp. 59–61, p. 66 above.

ent sort has been fought over his statements on the doctrine of original sin. No less an expert on this doctrine than Augustine said that Cyprian and his colleagues had stated the doctrine "in such a way as if by divine providence the Catholic Church were already confuting the Pelagian heretics who were to appear so much later."[13]

But the place of Cyprian in the Augustinian case against Pelagianism, and thus in the development of the Western doctrine of original sin, is not simply a position of honor. For Cyprian was, together with Ambrose,[14] the chief proof in Augustine's anti-Pelagian writings, that his doctrine of original sin was not an innovation of his own, but had the right to claim the supporting authority of earlier dogmatic tradition. As Bonner suggests, "it is with obvious delight that he quotes St. Cyprian for the benefit of an African congregation."[15] Repeatedly Augustine attacked Pelagius for "the innovation which is now beginning to raise its voice against the ancient, implanted opinion of the Church."[16] It was especially from the writings of Cyprian, which were in turn informed by even earlier tradition, that Augustine sought to prove that "what we hold is the true, the truly Christian, and the Catholic faith, as it was handed down of old through the Sacred Scriptures, and so retained and preserved by our fathers and to this very time, in which these men have attempted to overthrow it."[17]

The provocation for this defense was the repeated charge of Pelagius and his supporters that the tradition of the

13. Augustine, *Contra duas epistolas Pelagianorum* iv.23, *CSEL 60*, 546–47.

14. Ibid. iv.29–32, *CSEL 60*, 559–69.

15. Gerald Bonner, *St. Augustine of Hippo: Life and Controversies* (London, 1963), p. 319.

16. Augustine, *De peccatorum meritis et remissione* iii.6, *CSEL 60*, 132.

17. Augustine, *Contra duas epistolas Pelagianorum* iv.32, *CSEL 60*, 568.

Church was on their side in the opposition to Augustine's view of the fall of Adam. Sometimes this charge took the form of the *ad hominem* accusation that Augustine's doctrine was a vestigial remnant of his days as a Manichaean heretic. "Anyone who defends [the doctrine of] original evil is a thoroughgoing Manichaean," said Augustine's Pelagian opponent.[18] Augustine replied that heresy, by emphasizing one aspect of Catholic doctrine at the expense of others, was bound to mistake orthodoxy for the heresy of the opposite extreme; thus "just as the Arians accuse us of being Sabellians . . . so the Pelagians throw the Manichaeans up to us."[19] Occasionally Augustine felt compelled to admit that earlier Christian teachers had not confronted the question of grace, predestination, and free will in the form in which it had now been posed. "Before this heresy [Pelagianism] arose, they did not have the necessity to deal with this question, so difficult of solution. They would undoubtedly have done so if they had been compelled to respond to such men."[20]

Still another defense put forth by Augustine was an admission that his own earlier views on the controverted issues had been inadequate and that his thought had undergone a development.[21] In his response to the accusation of Manichaeism, in his recognition that the orthodox tradition had not developed an adequate formulation of the doctrines at issue because it had not yet been challenged by the Pelagian heresy, and in his admission that his own thought as ex-

18. Quoted in Augustine, *De nuptiis et concupiscentia* ii.49, *CSEL 42*, 304; cf. Joseph Rickaby, *The Manichees as Saint Augustine Saw Them* (London, 1925), pp. 19–23.
19. Augustine, *De nuptiis et concupiscentia* ii.38, *CSEL 42*, 292.
20. Augustine, *De praedestinatione sanctorum* xiv.27, *PL 44*, 980.
21. Augustine, *De dono perseverantiae* xxi.55, *PL 45*, 1027.

pressed in his early books had been underdeveloped and incomplete, Augustine drew upon the writings of Cyprian for substantiation and support. If Augustine and his Catholic allies were Manichaeans in teaching their doctrine of original sin, "will anyone [dare to] say of Cyprian, with his crown of transcendent glory, that he was or even could have been a Manichaean?"[22]

Even though earlier commentators on Scripture had not recognized all the implications of certain crucial biblical passages, such as Wisdom 4:11 ("He was caught up lest evil change his understanding or guile deceive his soul."[23]). Cyprian's treatise *On the Mortality* was one evidence that Augustine's interpretation of death, citing this very passage, stood in the succession of the orthodox Catholic tradition.[24] And although he claimed that he had "now stated [the doctrine of perseverance] in a way in which no one before me has stated it,"[25] he did find a precedent for his language in Cyprian's exposition *On the Lord's Prayer*.[26]

Augustine's use of the theology of Cyprian to vindicate his orthodoxy against the Pelagian charge of doctrinal novelty must be seen in the context of his even more extensive discussion of Cyprian's theology in the controversy with the Donatists.[27] They had demanded that anyone who had been baptized by a heretical or a morally compromised bishop be

22. Augustine, *De nuptiis et concupiscentia* ii.51, *CSEL 42*, 307–08.

23. On the use of this passage in Cyprian's *De mortalitate*, and in the thought of other early church fathers, cf. Jaroslav Pelikan, *The Shape of Death: Life, Death, and Immortality in the Early Fathers* (New York, 1961), pp. 55–73, esp. pp. 66–67; also pp. 25–26, 106–07.

24. Augustine, *De praedestinatione sanctorum* xiv.26–28, *PL 44*, 979–81.

25. Augustine, *De dono perseverantiae* xxi.55, *PL 45*, 1027.

26. Cyprian, *De dominica oratione* 12–27, *CSEL 3*, Pt. I, 274–87.

27. See pp. 66–67, n. 82 above.

rebaptized upon his return to the fellowship of the true Church, and in support of their demand they cited the authority of Cyprian, who had espoused a similar doctrine in opposition to Pope Stephen I. Consequently, they accused Augustine of betraying the doctrinal tradition of the North African bishop and martyr, Cyprian. Augustine's reply to the Donatists was to appeal from Cyprian's doctrine of baptism and consequent practice of rebaptism to Cyprian's doctrine of the Church and of its unity. Cyprian's fundamental loyalty, Augustine argued, was to the one Church of Christ, the seamless robe which none dared to tear apart.[28] And so it was more faithful to the heritage of Cyprian for the Catholics to maintain the unity of the Spirit in the bond of peace than for the Donatists to insist upon rebaptism at the expense of unity.[29]

CYPRIAN ON INFANT BAPTISM

Of all the many passages Augustine quoted from Cyprian in defense of his doctrine against the Pelagians, none was as important to him as the letter now known as epistle 64 of Cyprian.[30] Augustine quoted it against the Pelagians over and over, and even called it Cyprian's "book on the baptism of infants."[31] There seems to be no way to fix the date

28. Cyprian, *De catholicae ecclesiae unitate* 7, CSEL 3, Pt. I, 215; cf. Willis, *Saint Augustine and the Donatist Controversy*, pp. 146–52.

29. I hope sometime to examine "Augustine's Cyprian" in more detail as a study in the problem of development of doctrine and the continuity of the Church, for Cyprian's doctrine of baptism was a fundamental issue common both to the controversy with Donatism and to the conflict with Pelagianism.

30. Cyprian, *Epistolae* lxiiii, CSEL 3, Pt. II, 717–21.

31. Augustine, *De nuptiis et concupiscentia* ii.51, CSEL 42, 308. Cf. J. B. Bord, "L'autorité de S. Cyprien dans la controverse baptismale jugée d'après S. Augustin," *Revue d'histoire ecclésiastique, 18* (1922), 455–68.

of the epistle, which, as we shall see, may have some relevance to its doctrine of original sin; it suffices to note that it seems to have been written some time after the second of the councils convoked to deal with the problem of the lapsed, thus after 252 and in the last years of Cyprian's life.[32] Because of its importance, the crucial passage of the epistle deserves to be quoted in full:

> If, when they subsequently come to believe, forgiveness of sins is granted even to the worst transgressors and to those who have sinned much against God, and if no one is denied access to baptism and to grace; how much less right do we have to deny it to an infant, who, having been born recently, has not sinned, except in that, being born physically according to Adam, he has contracted the contagion of the ancient death by his first birth. [The infant] approaches that much more easily to the reception of the forgiveness of sins because the sins remitted to him are not his own, but those of another.[33]

Some scholars have commented on how Augustinian this sounds, and indeed the passage is actually cited or quoted by Augustine in several places.[34] In addition, there is an evident parallel between the phrase of Cyprian, "secundum

32. See Hugo Koch, "Abfassungszeit und Veranlassung der cyprianischen Schriften De lapsis und De ecclesiae unitate," *Cyprianische Untersuchungen*, pp. 79–82.

33. "Porro autem si etiam grauissimis delictoribus et in Deum multum ante peccantibus, cum postea crediderint, remissa peccatorum datur et a baptismo adque gratia nemo prohibetur, quanto magis prohiberi non debet infans qui recens natus nihil peccavit, nisi quod secundum Adam carnaliter natus contagium mortis antiquae prima natiuitate contraxit, qui ad remissam peccatorum accipiendam hoc ipso facilius accedit quod illi remittuntur non propria, sed aliena peccata." Cyprian, *Epistolae* lxiiii.5, *CSEL 3*, Pt. II, 720–21.

34. Augustine, *De peccatorum meritis et remissione* iii.10, *CSEL 60*, 135–37; *Contra duas epistolas Pelagianorum* iv.23, *CSEL 60*, 546–47.

Adam *carnaliter* natus *contagium* mortis antiquae prima natiuitate *contraxit*," and a phrase of Augustine in his treatise *On Original Sin,* "debitum quod *contagio carnalis* generationis *attraxit*."[35] It certainly does not seem far-fetched to suggest that Cyprian's words probably contributed their distinctive form and vocabulary to Augustine as he wrote this passage.

Turning to a close reading of Cyprian's words themselves, we should note that he was not speaking on his own behalf as a bishop, much less as a theologian, but in the name of a solemn conclave of churchmen. The salutation of the epistle in the existing manuscripts speaks of "Cyprian and other colleagues, 66 in number, who attended the council."[36] The epistle had been called forth by the questions raised in the practice of Fidus, who thought that the eighth day after the birth of a child was time enough for it to be baptized, but "it seemed far different in our council."[37] What Cyprian was arguing was not his own doctrine but rather that on which "all of us have rendered a judgment." The conclusion of the epistle reiterated that "this was our opinion in our council,"[38] thus confirming the authoritative claim of the epistle upon its reader. Here spoke not the opinion of any individual bishop—for, as Cyprian's attitude toward Stephen, bishop of Rome, suggests, no amount of antiquity could give such authority to any one see[39]—but

35. Augustine, *De gratia Christi et de peccato originali* ii.37, *CSEL 42,* 196; italics, of course, are mine.

36. Cyprian, *Epistolae* lxiiii.1, *CSEL 3,* Pt. II, 717.

37. Ibid. lxiiii.2, *CSEL 3,* Pt. II, 718.

38. Ibid. lxiiii.6, *CSEL 3,* Pt. II, 721.

39. Cf. Bernhard Poschmann, *Ecclesia principalis: Zur Frage des Primats bei Cyprian* (Breslau, 1933); and Hugo Koch, *Cathedra Petri: Neue Untersuchungen über die Anfänge der Primatslehre* (Giessen, 1930), pp. 32–154.

a corporate judgment of a properly convoked council, albeit a local one, since all councils before Nicaea were local or at most regional.

It is evident, moreover, that the bishops believed themselves to be speaking in the name of the universal Church ahd of its doctrine and practice. Although the North African synod was local, Cyprian's attitude toward the synods dealing with the lapsed, in which he had participated, suggests that he regarded the decisions even of such synods as binding upon others. For that reason he could write, after stating such a decision, that anyone who disagreed with it would have to "render an account to the Lord in the day of judgment, either for his rash censure or for his inhuman hardness."[40]

Disagreement among the bishops of the Church Catholic was not unknown to Cyprian; even the bishop of the most prestigious see in the Church was capable of error, at least in judgment. But when Cyprian enunciated his doctrine of original sin in the context of pastoral counsel on the practical question of when infants should be baptized—when they should be baptized, not whether they should, the choice being between the eighth day of life and an earlier time—it was much more than his own theories that he propounded, and the "we" of the epistle was not simply a literary device.

A Maiori ad Minus

Cyprian's epistle was not called forth by the problem of infant baptism alone. He had also been concerned by the scandal of the lax practice of Therapius, a bishop who had

40. Cyprian, *Epistolae* lvii.5, *CSEL* 3, Pt. 11, 655.

granted reconciliation and fellowship to Victor, a former presbyter, contrary to the standards laid down by the councils of the Church for such cases.[41] In this present context we need not trace the evolution of Cyprian's attitude toward the lapsed, from the typically North African rigorism of his early years through the adjustments imposed by pastoral duty to the more evangelical doctrine at work in his maturer practice.[42] But penitential practice does provide part of the setting for his doctrines both of infant baptism and of original sin. At the risk of oversystematization, one might say that in the inchoate sacramental theology of Cyprian, baptism was to original sin as penance was to actual sin. More precisely, Cyprian developed his doctrine of the original sin remitted in baptism not simply by analogy with the actual sin remitted in penance but by the contrast between original sin and actual sin. He demonstrated his doctrine by arguing a maiori ad minus.

The "maius" of the case was the missionary practice of the Church, which invited all to participate in the grace of God, regardless of how grievously they had sinned before. "If anything could hinder men from obtaining grace, their graver sins could rather hinder those who are adult and mature and older," Cyprian argued.[43] But in fact these sins, even the graver sins of those who were "adult and mature and older," did not disqualify sinners from being converted and receiving the grace of God. The case of Christians who had fallen was, of course, different. They could not be dealt

41. As we have noted on p. 79, the incident and the epistle cannot be dated precisely.

42. Cf. Koch, "Die Bussfrage bei Cyprian," *Cyprianische Untersuchungen,* pp. 211–85.

43. Cyprian, *Epistolae* lxiiii.5, *CSEL 3,* Pt. II, 720.

with as though they had never been enlightened by conversion and baptism. Therefore, they were not simply sinners but traitors, not simply penitents but "lapsed."[44] The epistle was explicit in declaring that a premature readmission of one such lapsed, the presbyter Victor, "rather disturbed us,"[45] for it appeared to be lowering the bars sooner and more easily than Cyprian and his colleagues, even after the controversy over the lapsed, were prepared to do. Nevertheless, they counseled that the *pax,* once properly even though prematurely granted by a bishop, should not be withdrawn.

All the more amazing, argued Cyprian, was it that where access to the *pax* of the Church and to the grace of God had been conferred upon a sinner after less than adequate satisfaction, there should arise the question of whether children should have to wait eight days before being granted such access. For if pagans, after having committed actual sins that were truly grave, could be reconciled with God; and if even believers who had been guilty of mortal sins could finally achieve reconciliation after due repentance and proper satisfaction—how much more ready must the Church be to admit to grace those whose only burden was the sin of Adam! The sins of which the pagans and the lapsed were absolved were their own sins, consciously and even deliberately committed. The sins of the infants were those of another, or of others; they had not yet sinned in their own name. This did not necessarily mean that original sin was less grave than actual sin; it was still a "contagion." But it did mean that original sin by itself was less grave than original sin compounded by actual sins. If the latter condition did not bar

44. Cf. Cyprian, *De lapsis, CSEL 3,* Pt. I, 235–64.
45. Cyprian, *Epistolae* lxiiii.1, *CSEL 3,* Pt. II, 717.

a person from grace, it was clear to Cyprian that the formerly certainly should not.

Argument A Fortiori

In addition to this definition, a maiori ad minus, a second line of development in Cyprian's statement of the doctrine of original sin on the basis of infant baptism was an a fortiori argument, based on the relation between the Old Testament and the New. In the Old Testament, circumcision had been required on the eighth day after birth. This was a "sacrament given previously in shadow and in image; but with the coming of Christ, it was completed in truth."[46] Daniélou and others have shown the great contribution made by the typological exegesis of the Old Testament to the development of the Christian doctrine of baptism, concentrating especially on the Flood and the Exodus as types of baptism in the theology of the fathers, including Cyprian.[47] Circumcision was, if anything, even more prominent in what Lundberg has called "baptismal typology."[48] Cyprian's *Three Books of Testimonies Against the Jews* developed the typology in two theses, asserting both that the first circumcision, that of the flesh, had been superseded by the circumcision of the spirit,[49] and that the baptism adumbrated in the Old Testament had now been instituted by the coming of Christ.[50] The *Testimonies* also drew the contrast between the Old Testament *signaculum*, which "does

46. Ibid. lxiiii 4, *CSEL 3*, Pt. II, 719–20.
47. Daniélou, *From Shadows to Reality*, pp. 98–99, 195–96.
48. P. Lundberg, *La typologie baptismale dans l'ancienne Église* (Lund, 1942).
49. Cyprian, *Ad Quirinum Testimonia* i.8, *CSEL 3*, Pt. I, 45–46.
50. Ibid. i.12, *CSEL 3*, Pt. I, 47.

not benefit women,"[51] and the new Testament *signum Domini,* by which "all are signed."[52]

That typology of adumbration and fulfillment appears to underlie Cyprian's formulation in his epistle on infant baptism and original sin. Circumcision had been instituted for a particular group in a particular nation, as part of the covenant of God with the old Israel and of the law given to Abraham and to Moses. But now the "former law" was to cease and to be replaced by a "new law"; "another dispensation" and a "new covenant" were being promulgated.[53] One "new" feature of this new law and new covenant was universality, for the barren synagogue had now given way to a fruitful mother who was to have many children, the Church with her children from among the Gentiles.[54] If, even under the old covenant and old law, the *signaculum* of circumcision was to be administered on the eighth day, the fulfillment that had come in Christ and the universality of his grace surely required that the *signum* of baptism be administered even sooner. Cyprian and his colleagues concluded, therefore, that the "law already promulgated" was not to be permitted to keep anyone from grace, but that "absolutely everyone should be admitted to the grace of Christ."[55]

Proceeding in a similar fashion, Joachim Jeremias has argued on the basis of Colossians 2:11 that in the early Church the Jewish practice of proselyte circumcision

51. If, that is, the reading *feminis* (which makes more sense) is the right one, in preference to *seminis* (which may be textually better attested).

52. Cyprian, *Ad Quirinum Testimonia* i.8, CSEL 3, Pt. I, 46.

53. Ibid. i.9–11, CSEL 3, Pt. I, 46–47.

54. Ibid. i.20–21, CSEL 3, Pt. I, 52–57.

55. Cyprian, *Epistolae* lxiiii.5, CSEL 3, Pt. II, 720.

provided a justification for the baptism of both adults and infants upon the conversion of a family to Christianity.[56] As Jeremias also points out, however, the idea of baptizing children "for the forgiveness of sins" raised a serious question for Origen.[57] Origen answered the question of "Whose sins?" by hinting at, but certainly not by formulating, a doctrine of original sin. Other scholars have also commented on the vagueness of Origen's justification for the practice of infant baptism.[58] Cyprian would thus appear to have been the first teacher of the Church to connect an explicit argument for the baptism of infants with an explicit statement of the doctrine that, through their physical birth, children inherited the sins of Adam and the death that was the wages of sin.

Both Origen and Cyprian accepted infant baptism as a given element of the sacramental practice of the Church; both were asking the question, "Whose sins?" But Cyprian answered the question by formulating a doctrine of original sin. It seems, then, that the sacramental practice came first in the history of the Church, and that there followed "discussions among Christians, not indeed about the fact of infant baptism, but rather about the reason for it."[59] A study of Cyprian suggests the conclusion that he developed his doctrine of original sin from the existing practice of the Church a posteriori, to make the diagnosis fit the cure.

56. Joachim Jeremias, *Infant Baptism in the First Five Centuries*, trans. David Cairns (London, 1960), pp. 39–40.

57. Origen, *Homiliae super Lucam* xiv.5, *GCS 49*, 87–88.

58. Jeremias, p. 65; Ph. H. Menoud, "Le baptême des enfants dan l'Église ancienne," *Verbum Caro*, 2 (1948), 15–26.

59. Henri Crouzel, François Fournier, and Pierre Périchon, ed., Origene, *Homélies sur S. Luc*, Sources chrétiennes 87 (Paris, 1962), 222–23, n. 2.

THE SIGNIFICANCE OF TERTULLIAN

But, to recur to the problem with which we began, why should the doctrine of original sin have developed in the West before it developed in the East, and not have developed even in the West until Cyprian? A decisive part of any historical answer to this question, as to so many other questions about the development of doctrine in the West before Augustine, is the thought of Tertullian. In his writings alone at that time, according to Newman's *Essay on Development,* "the two antagonist principles of dogmatism and development are found . . . though with some deficiency of amalgamation, and with a greater leaning towards the dogmatic."[60] Tertullian either created or codified formulas that were to become the standard dogmatic language of the Latin Church throughout its history.

The careful probing by two generations of scholars into the thought and the language of Tertullian now makes it possible for us to summarize his doctrine of the fall.[61] In his *Exhortation to Chastity,* Tertullian called Adam "the pioneer of our race and of our sin."[62] Elsewhere he spoke of "that state which Adam had lost when he transgressed."[63] And against Marcion he stated that "man is condemned to death for having tasted the fruit of one miserable tree, and from it proceed sins with their penalties; and now all are perishing who have never even seen a single bit of Paradise."[64] These statements, which could easily be multiplied,

60. Newman, *Essay,* p. 349.
61. Cf. Johannes Quasten, *Patrology* (Westminster, Md., 1951 ff.), 2, 246–340, where much of this literature is cited and summarized.
62. Tertullian, *De exhortatione castitatis* ii.5, *CC, SL* 2, 1017.
63. Tertullian, *De pudicitia* ix.16, *CC, SL,* 2, 1298.
64. Tertullian, *Adversus Marcionem* i.22, *CC, SL* 1, 464.

would seem to corroborate the conclusion of a recent manual that from the teaching of Tertullian, "it is a short step . . . to the doctrine of original sin."[65]

Short step or not, there were at least two obstacles between Tertullian's thought and the ecclesiastical doctrine of original sin. One was his view of the soul; the other was his rejection of infant baptism. Tertullian could speak as he did about the transmission of sin from Adam to the subsequent generations of the human race at least partly because he interpreted the soul as a quasi-physical constituent of man's nature.[66] Drawing upon the medical information available to him, including among others the writings of the pagan physician, Soranus of Ephesus, Tertullian taught that the seed of the soul was passed on from father to child just as the seed of the body was. Both the body and the soul "are conceived and put together and perfected simultaneously, as well as born together."[67] Thus both the soul and the body had come down from Adam to all men, having been present in him; and "every soul, by reason of its birth, is regarded as [still existing] in Adam until it is reborn in Christ."[68]

But Tertullian does not seem to have admitted that the soul was "reborn" through infant baptism. "Why should innocent infancy be in such a hurry to come to the forgiveness of sins?" he asked in his treatise on baptism. He replied: "Let them come while they are maturing, while they are learning, while they are being taught what it is they are

65. J. N. D. Kelly, *Early Christian Doctrines* (New York, 1958), p. 175.
66. Cf. Heinrich Karpp, *Probleme altchristlicher Anthropologie* (Gütersloh, 1950), pp. 41–91.
67. Tertullian, *De anima* xxvii.1, in *Quinti Septimi Florentis Tertulliani De anima*, ed. J. H. Waszink (Amsterdam, 1947), p. 38; commentary, pp. 342–48.
68. Ibid. xl.1, p. 56; commentary, pp. 448–49.

coming to. Let them be made Christians when they have become able to know Christ."[69] And so the "short step" to the doctrine of original sin may not have been so short after all; for as Ernest Evans comments, Tertullian "could hardly have taken this attitude . . . unless he had held lightly to the doctrine of original sin."[70]

Although Cyprian does not seem to have referred to Tertullian by name in his writings, he was deeply indebted to his North African predecessor. According to the well-known account of Jerome, Cyprian "made it a practice never to pass a day without reading Tertullian, and he would frequently say to his secretary, 'Hand me the master,' meaning by this, Tertullian."[71] The implications of this account have been examined by several meticulous studies which have traced the literary dependence upon Tertullian of various books by Cyprian.[72] For example, Cyprian's *On the Good of Patience* seems to show extensive reliance on the corresponding work by Tertullian.[73] On the other hand, Cyprian's *On the Lord's Prayer* is relatively independent of Tertullian's *On Prayer*.[74] Historians have sometimes tended to identify Cyprian's thought with Tertullian's more closely than the facts warrant and to overlook the striking differences between them. The most far-reaching difference is probably that which separates the Montanist sectarianism

69. Tertullian, *De Baptismo* xviii.5, *CC, SL, 1*, 293.

70. Ernest Evans, ed., *Tertullian's Homily on Baptism* (London, 1964), p. 101.

71. Jerome, *De viris illustribus* liii, *PL 23*, 698.

72. Cf. Quasten, 2, 340–64.

73. Mary George Edward Conway, "Saint Cyprian and Tertullian," *Thasci Caecilii Cypriani De Bono Patientiae* (Washington, 1957), pp. 18–45.

74. Cf. Clement Maria O'Donnell, "Literary Dependence on Tertullian," *St. Cyprian on the Lord's Prayer* (Washington, 1960), pp. 28–38.

of Tertullian from the Catholic churchmanship of Cyprian, for this affected such doctrines as the ministry and penance. It also affected the evident difference between the two men on the practice of infant baptism and hence on the doctrine of original sin.

The practice of infant baptism was in Christian usage at Tertullian's time, as at Cyprian's; but Tertullian attacked the practice while Cyprian affirmed it and argued on the basis of it. Tertullian was a more able and more creative theologian than Cyprian. But Tertullian's own intuitions in the direction of the doctrine of original sin did not in fact develop into that doctrine, while it was the more prosaic and derivative theology of Cyprian that formulated what was to become, through Augustine, the doctrine of the Western Church. All three methods of development of doctrine to which we have referred—a maiori ad minus, as applied to the missionary practice of the Church and its pastoral administration of penance; a fortiori, as applied to the contrast between circumcision and baptism; and a posteriori, as applied to the practice of infant baptism—were, in fact, the fruits not of the cleverness of Cyprian as an individual theologian but of the continuing life and corporate experience of the Church. Nor did the doctrine of baptism and the doctrine of original sin emerge merely, or even primarily, from the Church's reflection on other doctrines. They came rather from a deepening awareness of what the coming of Christ meant for the life of the Church and for its mission.

EASTERN AND WESTERN VIEWS

The doctrine of original sin arose within the theological heritage of Tertullian because he seems to have been the first post-apostolic writer to give concentrated attention to the fateful consequences of man's first disobedience.[75] Until that disobedience was seen as something more profound than an evil example, it was virtually impossible to avoid a superficial and moralistic view of the fall of Adam. Tertullian was aided in his discovery of the more profound implications of the fall by his quasi-materialistic definition of the soul, which, whatever its disadvantages may have been for a sensitive interpretation of human psychology, could at least affirm the solidarity of the human species both in its origins and in its guilt. But because Tertullian's definition of fall and sin was not shaped simultaneously by an acceptance of the Church's practice of infant baptism, it did not develop into a doctrine of original sin.[76]

The tradition of the East had developed its own views of sin and death, many of which were less preoccupied with the notion of punishment than those that have characterized Latin theology.[77] Indeed, one such view, the idea that death represented a divine deliverance from the continuing power of sin, was so completely an Eastern view of sin and death that its occurrence in the thought of Cyprian created something of an embarrassment for Augustine.[78] Yet the Augustinian view of original sin and death, which has so easily fallen into the perennial heresy of Jansenism, required the

75. Karpp, pp. 62–63.

76. Thus I cannot agree with the ideas of "hellenization" expressed by Karl Emmel, *Das Fortleben der antiken Lehren von der Beseelung bei den Kirchenvätern* (Leipzig, 1918), pp. 42 ff.

77. John S. Romanides, "Man and his True Life according to the Greek Orthodox Service Book," *The Greek Orthodox Theological Review, I* (1954), 63–83, esp. 70–72.

78. Augustine, *De praedestinatione sanctorum* xiv.26, PL *44*, 979–80.

corrective supplied by the Eastern view, which saw death as pedagogical rather than punitive in the divine plan.[79]

The difference could not help but affect both the form and the rate of doctrinal development in these two parts of the Church. It also helps to explain why Pelagius managed to persuade a group of Eastern bishops that he was not a heretic, for he affirmed both the necessity of divine grace and the free will of man in a manner that Eastern theology and piety found congenial. Eventually the understanding of the person and work of Christ implied in the thought of a Greek theologian such as Gregory of Nyssa would seem to presuppose a conception of sin, death, and finitude that would include not only man but the entire creation, and therefore it would appear to demand a doctrine of original sin even more penetrating than the Augustinian.[80] The development of such a doctrine—existentially more pessimistic, but essentially more optimistic—is a part of the history of Christian thought in the Greek tradition.[81]

It fell to the Latin tradition, however, to formulate the

79. On the contrast between the Augustinian doctrine of man and the Eastern view, see Vasily Zenkowsky, *Das Bild vom Menschen in der Ostkirche* (Stuttgart, 1951).

80. Cf. Ernest V. McClear, "The Fall of Man and Original Sin in the Theology of Gregory of Nyssa," *Theological Studies, 9* (1948), 175–212. Father McClear seems to me, however, to make less of the differences between Gregory of Nyssa and Augustine than the texts warrant, as I have sought to show, without explicitly referring to McClear, in my Ingersoll Lecture, delivered at Harvard University on May 2, 1963, and published as "The Mortality of God and the Immortality of Man in Gregory of Nyssa" in Philip J. Hefner, ed., *The Scope of Grace: Essays on Nature and Grace in Honor of Joseph Sittler* (Philadelphia, 1964), pp. 77–97.

81. For a contemporary effort to exploit the distinct emphases of the Greek Christian tradition, cf. John Hick, *Evil and the God of Love* (New York, 1966), pp. 207–24.

ecclesiastical doctrine of original sin in the form in which it has entered into the dogmatic language of Christendom. And it was Cyprian, the defender of the unity of the Church Catholic, who articulated this doctrine in a formula that came to be recognized as both novel in its language and orthodox in its meaning, thus expressing simultaneously the continuity of the Christian faith and the development of doctrine.

4
Athanasius on Mary

The author of the *Essay on Development* turned to the problem of development of doctrine both because it had become central in his personal religious struggle and because it was unavoidable in his historical studies. Almost exclusively patristic, these studies were centered on the thought and writings of Athanasius, "toward whom," as Jean Guitton says, "Newman always maintained a kind of reverence."[1] Newman's first book had been *The Arians of the Fourth Century*, originally published in 1833; Athanasius was its hero, one of those whose works "evince gifts, moral and intellectual, of so high a cast, as to render it a privilege to be allowed to sit at the feet of their authors, and to receive the words, which they have been, as it were, commissioned to deliver."[2] A few years later Newman turned to an even more careful study of those words, undertaking a translation of selected writings of Athanasius.[3] On December 21, 1841, he reported that he had been working at the first proofs of the translation for three months "at the rate of from eight to twelve hours a day [I wrote the notes to the text already in type], yet have done so little as to be

1. Jean Guitton, *La philosophie de Newman: Essai sur l'idée de développement* (Paris, 1933), p. 3.
2. Newman, *The Arians of the Fourth Century*, p. v.
3. The translation appeared as Volumes 8 and 19 of A Library of the Fathers of the Holy Catholic Church Anterior to the Division of the East and West (London, 1842 and 1844), under the title *Select Treatises of S. Athanasius, Archbishop of Alexandria, in Controversy with the Arians*.

almost ashamed to make this avowal."[4] But on November 24, 1844, he was able to write to his sister that "the translation of St. Athanasius is, I am glad to say, just coming to an end, and I shall (so be it) relax."[5]

The form which this relaxation took was the *Essay on the Development of Christian Doctrine,* which he had already begun to work on in March of 1844. Athanasius was to be Newman's companion for most of his life, and in 1881 he published a new translation of the three *Orations Against the Arians* which was in many ways more a paraphrase than a translation and which therefore often tells one more about Newman than about Athanasius.[6] It is chiefly on his work as an editor and translator of Athanasius that Newman's claim to historical scholarship must rest. It is also from that work that much of his firsthand acquaintance with the development of doctrine was derived. Certainly the most arresting reference to Athanasius in the *Essay on Development* is the flat statement that "St. Athanasius' condemnation of their [the Arians'] theology is a vindication of the Medieval."[7] The context of this remark is a discussion of the development of the doctrine of Mary.

CONTROVERSY BETWEEN EAST AND WEST

The doctrine of Mary constitutes a very special and difficult case of doctrinal development, and as such a case it

4. J. H. Newman to J. W. Bowden, St. Thomas' Day [December 21], 1841, *Letters and Correspondence of John Henry Newman During His Life in the English Church,* ed. Anne Mozley (2 vols. London, 1891), 2, 376.

5. J. H. Newman to Mrs. J. Mozley, November 24, 1844, ibid., p. 445.

6. *Select Treatises of St. Athanasius in Controversy with the Arians,* freely translated with an appendix by John Henry Cardinal Newman (2 vols. 8th impression, London, 1900).

7. Newman, *Essay,* p. 406.

occupies a special place in the history of the controversy between Roman Catholicism and Protestantism over the propriety of "new doctrines." It also occupies a special place
in the history of the controversy between the Greek East
and the Latin West.

The differences in development of the doctrine of Mary
in the East and in the West were the subject of occasional
warnings by Latin churchmen. Thus a sermon of Peter
Chrysologus, bishop of Ravenna in the first half of the fifth
century, attacked "those who have endeavored to becloud
Latin purity with a Greek thunderstorm" regarding the
proper titles for the Virgin Mary.[8] These sentiments and
some of these very words were echoed in one of the most
influential documents on the doctrine of Mary in the Middle
Ages, the letter *Cogitis Me,* published as Epistle IX of the
"supposed works" of Jerome but probably composed by
Radbertus in the ninth century.[9]

> Because there are many Easterners going about covered
> with their own filth, you should be put on guard, lest they
> becloud you with the darkness of their smooth talk or
> bemuse [your] Latin purity with [their] Greek confusion.
> For there are wise virgins, but there are also foolish ones.
> And therefore, my beloved, imitate the blessed and glori-
> ous Virgin whom you love and whose festival you are cele-
> brating today.[10]

8. Peter Chrysologus, *Sermones* cxlv, *PL 52,* 590.

9. On the authorship of the *Cogitis Me,* cf. the summary discussion of
Martin Jugie, *La mort et l'assomption de la Sainte Vierge: Étude historico-
doctrinale,* Studi e testi (Vatican City, 1944), p. 278, n. 2, and the literature
cited there; also H. Barré, "La lettre du Pseudo-Jérôme sur l'Assomption
est-elle antérieure à Paschase Radbert?" *Revue Bénédictine, 68* (1958), 203–25.

10. Pseudo-Jerome, *Epistolae* ix.13, *PL 30,* 136.

The irony of this attack is that the very themes whose "Latin purity" these authors wanted to defend against "Greek confusion" came not from the West and the Latins, but from the East and the Greeks. In fact, the closing admonition of *Cogitis Me*—to imitate the Virgin and to celebrate her festival—summarizes quite succinctly the significance of Athanasius, one of the Greeks, for the development of the doctrine of Mary. It is interesting, moreover, that although there is a substantial study by Soell on the mariology of the Cappadocian fathers,[11] the only special investigation of Athanasius' teaching on the subject seems to be a brief and quite speculative essay by Sergei Bulgakov.[12]

The position of Athanasius in the development of the doctrine of Mary is an ambiguous one. He was, in the words of one patristic scholar, "astonishingly noncommittal"[13] on the question of her perpetual virginity, at least in the writings preserved as the traditional Athanasian corpus. In the *Second Oration Against the Arians*, Athanasius did speak of Christ's "taking flesh of Mary Ever-Virgin,"[14] but a variant text of the passage, preserved by Theodoret, reads simply "Virgin."[15] The other instances of the term "Ever-

11. G. Soell, "Die Mariologie der Kappadozier im Lichte der Dogmengeschichte," *Theologische Quartalschrift, 131* (1951), 163–88, 288–319, 426–57.

12. Sergei Bulgakov, "Učenie o Premudrosti Božiei u Sv. Afanasia Velikago i drugich otcov Cerkvi," appendix to his *Kupina neopalimaya* (Paris, 1927), pp. 261–288.

13. Walter J. Burghardt, "Mary in Eastern Patristic Thought" in Carol, *Mariology, 2,* 114.

14. Athanasius, *Oratio II. contra Arianos* 70, *PG 26,* 296.

15. Ibid., n. 20. Cf. Hans-Georg Opitz, *Untersuchungen zur Überlieferung der Schriften des Athanasius* (Berlin, 1935), pp. 153–55, on other variants in the version of Theodoret.

Virgin" in his works are either fragmentary or dubious or both.[16] When he defended the true humanity of Christ, in an epistle whose significance we shall weigh later in this chapter, he seems to have been arguing that while the conception of Jesus differed from normal conception because it took place without a human father, the birth itself was completely normal and identical with that of other men.[17] In his famous early essay *On the Incarnation of the Word of God,* moreover, he asserted that "when the Virgin was giving birth to him, it was not he [*autos*] who suffered or was stained by being in the body," as though to suggest that Mary did experience such a change.[18] Other passages from Athanasius, assembled by various scholars, confirm the impression "that the image of the spotlessly perfect, immaculate Virgin had not yet emerged in the mind of the fourth-century Fathers"[19] and seem to support the charge of "Greek confusion."

DEVELOPMENT BY EXTRAPOLATION

As a few scholars have recognized, the most productive place to look for mariology in the writings of Athanasius is not his polemical and theological output, but in his ascetical writings. Here he drew a parallel between Mary and the Christian virgin, just as he drew one between the heroic Christian ascetic, whose "soul was imperturbed and his outword appearance steady,"[20] and the heroic Christ, who, "im-

16. Pseudo-Athanasius, *Interpretatio in symbolum, PG 26,* 1232; Athanasius (?) *Fragmenta in Lucam* (a commentary on the Magnificat), *PG 27,* 1393.

17. Athanasius, *Epistola ad Epictetum 4, PG 26,* 1057.

18. Athanasius, *De incarnatione Verbi 17, PG 25,* 125.

19. Hilda Graef, *Mary: A History of Doctrine and Devotion 1* (New York, 1963), 53.

20. Athanasius, *Vita S. Antonii 67, PG 25,* 192.

passible and incorruptible and very Word [*Autologos*] and God maintained and saved in his own impassibility those suffering men for whose sakes he endured these things."[21] The use of the title *Christophoros* for the virgin Polycratia —he used it four times in all, never about a married person—also indicates that there was an analogy in his thought between Christ and the Christian ascetic.[22]

In his most elaborate explication of the related analogy between Mary and the Christian virgin, Athanasius also worked out his most detailed statement of the meaning of the virginity of Mary. It appears in a *Letter to the Virgins,* which has not been preserved in Greek but must be reconstructed from some Coptic fragments[23] and from the parallels between these and the Latin treatise *On the Virgins* of Ambrose of Milan.[24] A hazardous task of philological legerdemain in any case, this assignment is further complicated by the present state both of the manuscript evidence and of the scholarly debate on other ascetical writings of Athanasius, in particular the treatise *On Virginity,* the authenticity of which has been the subject of much controversy.[25]

But even proceeding with the greatest caution, we can see at work in the *Letter to the Virgins* the same use of the ascetic ideal that is present in the *Life of Saint Antony.* Not in his classic expositions of the deity of Christ and the incarnation, much less in any special dissertations on Mary, but in his letter of exhortation to "maidens who want to re-

21. Athanasius, *De incarnatione Verbi* 54, *PG* 25, 192.

22. Pelikan, *The Light of the World,* pp. 101–02.

23. *S. Athanase: Lettres festales et pastorales en Copte,* ed. L.-Th. Lefort, *CSCO* 150, 73–99 (Coptic); 151, 55–80 (French translation).

24. For the identification of these parallels I am indebted to Luigi Dossi, "S. Ambrogio e S. Atanasio nel de Virginibus," *Acme, 4* (1951), 241–62.

25. Quasten, *Patrology, 3,* 45–49.

main virgins and brides of Christ,"[26] Athanasius set forth
his fullest exposition of mariological teaching. When he told
the nuns that, as a principle of moral theology, they should
"learn to know [themselves] through her [Mary] as through
a mirror,"[27] the obverse method would therefore also appear to be a valid principle of his doctrinal theology: whatever were the distinguishing characteristics of the Christian
virgin who had been devoted to Christ ought to have been
even more distinctive of the character of the one who was
privileged to be the Virgin Mother of God. And the description of Mary in the *Letter to the Virgins* does indeed seem to
have been based on the life of Christian ascetics, a life of
modesty and service, of gentle words and steady progress in
charitable works, of preparation for heaven.

In the absence of biographical data about the life and person of the Virgin Mary in the gospels or in authenticated
tradition, Athanasius' doctrine seems to have turned for
information to the model of those who had found in her
"the image in accordance with which each one should fashion her own virginity." This procedure was quite in accordance with the teaching of Athanasius that "because of our
relationship [*syngeneia*] to his body we, too, have become
God's temple, and in consequence are made God's sons, in
such a way that even in us the Lord is now being worshiped."[28]

Such a method of what might be called development of
doctrine by extrapolation would seem to find at least part
of its justification in the understanding of the divine economy expressed by the concept of prophecy and fulfillment.

26. Athanasius, *Lettre aux Vierges*, CSCO 150, 77 (Coptic); 151, 59 (French).
27. Ibid., *CSCO* 150, 78 (Coptic); 151, 59 (French).
28. Athanasius, *Oratio I. contra Arianos* 43, *PG 26*, 100.

The Church and its theologians felt justified in drawing conclusions about the person and work of Christ from passages of the Old Testament, even when there was no corresponding statement in the New Testament.[29] The exegesis of the protevangel in Genesis 3:15—while certainly problematical in many ways[30]—does illustrate this method. It is noteworthy that, in his review of biblical texts dealing with the doctrine of Christ, Athanasius devoted more space to the eighth chapter of the Book of Proverbs than to any other passage, expounding it in detail through most of his *Second Oration Against the Arians*[31] and finding in it a fuller explanation of the relation between the Son of God and the creation than that provided by New Testament passages such as the first chapter of the Gospel of John, which may themselves have been based on this chapter. In the light of Athanasius' concept of types, images, and metaphors,[32] it does not seem alien to his method for him to amplify the teachings of the New Testament on the basis of what had become explicit in the history of salvation since the New Testament, just as he amplified them on the basis of what had been implicit before the New Testament.

But the ideal of virginity had become explicit only in the East by this time, and only in the East therefore could it serve as the basis for the development of mariological doctrine. This does not mean that Christian doctrine in the West had not given any thought to the question of virginity; some Western theologians, notably Tertullian,

29. See p. 63.
30. See p. 19, n. 28.
31. Athanasius, *Oratio II. contra Arianos* 18–82, *PG 26*, 184–321.
32. Pelikan, *The Light of the World,* pp. 26–31, on his conception of *paradeigmata*.

had spoken of it at considerable length.[33] But there was no institutional embodiment of the ideal of virginity in the West until the time of Athanasius, no ascetic model in in the West such as Saint Antony in the East. The first such model for the West was—Saint Antony. There is some reason to believe that Athanasius may actually have composed his *Life of Saint Antony* in response to the request of Western monks for further information about the founder of Christian monasticism.[34] In any case, it was translated into Latin during the lifetime of Athanasius and circulated widely; an old manuscript of a contemporary Latin translation, not published until this century, was found in the chapter library at St. Peter's in Rome.[35] Moreover, as we have noted earlier, Athanasius' *Letter to the Virgins* provided most of the material for the treatise *On the Virgins* of Ambrose, which has been called the first "significant turning point in the Mariological consciousness of the West" in well over a century.[36] Athanasius was able to extrapolate from the ideal of the Christian virgin to the doctrine about Mary the Virgin because he had an empirical basis for such extrapolation in the nascent monachism of fourth-century Egypt.

Thus the *Letter to the Virgins* asserted that "Mary persevered in her virginity to the end. . . . She remained a

33. Cf. William P. Le Saint, ed., *Tertullian: Treatises on Marriage and Remarriage*, Ancient Christian Writers (Westminster, Md., 1956).

34. In the Latin translation by Evagrius, the *Vita S. Antonii* bears the heading "Athanasius episcopus ad peregrinos fratres" *(PG 26, 837)* which presumably refers to "brethren" in the West.

35. Cf. G. Garitte, *Un témoin important du texte de la Vie de S. Antoine par S. Athanase: La version latine inédite des Archives du Chapitre de Saint-Pierre à Rome* (Brussels, 1939).

36. Burghardt, "Mary in Western Patristic Thought" in Carol, *1*, 140.

Virgin perpetually, she who gave birth to God."[37] The words from the cross in John 19:27, "Behold, your mother!" entrusting Mary to the care of the disciple John, proved to Athanasius that she had not had any other children. But as he wrote, he had before him the model of Christian virgins who, patterning their vocations after the life of the Virgin, had vowed perpetual virginity. "She who gave birth to God" was properly called the Mother of God; but she was also "our sister,"[38] who was not too remote for imitation. There is some poignancy in a development of Christian doctrine on the basis of which the author of the epistle *Cogitis Me* could admonish his readers to shun "Greek confusion" and to "imitate the blessed and glorious Virgin whom you love" only because the Greek Christians of Alexandria had loved and imitated her first and had, through theologians such as Athanasius, begun to document both their imitation and the mariological doctrine that underlay it.

DEVOTION AND DOGMA

But the *Cogitis Me* went on to speak of a "festival" of Mary which "you are celebrating today." Whatever the festival may have been, it too was something that "Latin purity" had learned from "Greek confusion," and something about which the writings of Athanasius provide us with a few tantalizing bits of information. That information suggests two lines of doctrinal development: Athanasius was apparently the first theological writer who both used the title "Mother of God" for Mary and formulated a theological rationale that could justify it; and Athanasius

37. Athanasius, *Lettre aux Vierges*, CSCO 150, 77 (Coptic); 151, 59 (French).
38. Athanasius, *Epistola ad Epictetum* 7, PG 26, 1061.

may have been the first writer to argue in support of the motherhood of Mary on the basis of a festival of Mary.[39]

"Mother of God"

The origins of the title "Mother of God" are obscure; in spite of the diligence of Hugo Rahner and others,[40] there is no altogether incontestable evidence that it was used before the century of Athanasius, despite Newman's categorical claim that "the title *Theotocos,* or Mother of God, was familiar to Christians from primitive times."[41] What is clear is that the first completely authenticated instances of the use of this title come from the city of Athanasius. Alexander, his patron and immediate predecessor as bishop there, referred to Mary as *Theotokos,* "God-bearer," in his encyclical of ca. 319 about the heresy of Arius.[42] From various evidence, including the taunts of Julian the Apostate a few decades later about the term *Theotokos,*[43] it seems reasonable to conclude that the title already enjoyed widespread acceptance in the piety of the faithful at Alexandria and beyond. Whatever may be the validity of facile modern theories about "mother goddesses" of Graeco-Roman paganism and their supposed significance for the

39. Cf. Jugie, pp. 179–80.

40. Hugo Rahner, "Hippolyt von Rom als Zeuge für den Ausdruck Theotokos," *Zeitschrift für katholische Theologie 59* (1935), 73–81. See the discussion and bibliography in Burghardt, "Mary in Eastern Patristic Thought" in Carol, 2, 117, n. 147.

41. Newman, *Essay,* p. 407.

42. Alexander, *Epistola ad Alexandrum Constantinopolitanum* 12, PG *18,* 568.

43. Julian, *Against the Galileans* 262 D, in *The Works of the Emperor Julian,* ed. Wilmer Cave Wright, Loeb Classical Library (3 vols. London, 1923), *3,* 398.

development of Christian mariology,[44] the term *Theotokos* is apparently a Christian creation that arose in the language of Christian devotion to her as the mother of the divine Savior and eventually received its theological justification from the Church's clarification of what was implied by the orthodox witness to him.

That justification was supplied by Athanasius. It does indeed appear "inchoatively"[45] in his summary statement of "the scope and character of Holy Scripture," which "contains a double account [*diplē epangelia*] of the Savior: that he was God forever and is the Son, being Logos and Radiance and Wisdom of the Father; and that afterwards, taking flesh of a Virgin, Mary the *Theotokos*, for us, he was made man."[46] But the theological explanation of this "double account" goes well beyond this summary statement of the creed. Most of the recent controversy about the theology of Athanasius has dealt with the question of whether he ascribed a human soul to Christ or whether he shared the "Logos + flesh" schema of the incarnation which came to be identified with the Apollinarist heresy.[47] That controversy has sometimes tended to obscure, however, his pioneering work in the elaboration of the "communication of the properties [*antidosis tōn idiōmatōn*]"[48] the principle that,

44. See, for example, Arnold J. Toynbee, *A Study of History*, 7, Pt. B (New York, 1963), 717.

45. Burghardt, "Mary in Eastern Patristic Thought" in Carol, 2, 120.

46. Athanasius, *Oratio III. contra Arianos* 29, *PG 26*, 385.

47. The controversy is well summarized in Aloys Grillmeier, *Christ in Christian Tradition: From the Apostolic Age to Chalcedon (451)*, trans. J. S. Bowden (New York, 1965), pp. 193–219, where most of the recent literature is discussed.

48. Cf. A. Michel, "Idiomes (Communication des)," *Dictionnaire de Théologie catholique*, 7, Pt. I (Paris, 1927), 595–602.

as a consequence of the incarnation and the union of the divine and the human nature in the one person of Jesus Christ, it was legitimate to predicate human properties of the Logos and divine properties of the man Jesus.

As Aloys Grillmeier has suggested, it was not until the debates over the term *Theotokos* in the first quarter of the fifth century "that the discussion of the so-called *communicatio idiomatum* in Christ began in earnest," even though language suggestive of it "had been employed since the apostolic age without further thought."[49] The place of Athanasius in its development seems, however, to be somewhat more important than Grillmeier makes it. He points to passages in which Athanasius "obviously regards the Logos as the real personal agent in those acts which are decisive for redemption, the passion and death of Christ" and cites "expressions which describe the redemptive activity of the Logos according to the rules of the *communicatio idiomatum*."[50] But in a long passage in his first *Oration Against the Arians,* Athanasius discussed in detail the question of the propriety of ascribing change and exaltation to the divine Logos, who could not be changed and did not need to be exalted. His answer to the question was a paraphrase of Philippians 2:6–11:

As he, being the Logos and existing in the form of God, was always worshiped; so, being still the same though he became man and was called Jesus, he nevertheless has the whole creation under foot, and bending their knees to him in this name [Jesus], and confessing that the incarnation of the Logos and his undergoing death in the flesh

49. Grillmeier, p. 357.
50. Ibid., p. 200.

has not happened against the glory of his Godhead, but "to the glory of God the Father."[51]

Therefore when Athanasius spoke of the Logos "taking flesh of a Virgin, Mary the *Theotokos*,"[52] he was echoing the language of popular devotion; but he had already begun to provide the title with the very rationale that was to help defend it against attack half a century after his death. As Newman suggested in *The Arians of the Fourth Century*, the people were orthodox even when the bishops were not.[53] In his use of the *Theotokos*, as in his use of other titles and metaphors, Athanasius aligned himself with the orthodoxy of popular devotion and vindicated it. The idea of *lex orandi lex credendi*, that implicit in Christian worship there was a normative doctrinal content, seems to have been formulated shortly after the time of Athanasius,[54] but he evidently worked on the basis of some such idea.

"The Commemoration of Mary"

The normative content of devotion also became evident in another context, when Athanasius used the commemoration of Mary to vindicate the orthodoxy of his doctrine. He did so in at least two of his writings. The more important of these is his epistle to Epictetus, which was to achieve wide circulation in Greek, Latin, Syriac, and Armenian during

51. Athanasius, *Oratio I. contra Arianos* 42, *PG 26*, 100.

52. Athanasius, *Oratio III. contra Arianos* 29, *PG 26*, 385.

53. John Henry Newman, "The Orthodoxy of the Body of the Faithful during the Supremacy of Arianism," Note V to *The Arians of the Fourth Century* (3d ed. London, 1871), pp. 454–72; the Note originally appeared as a separate article in 1859.

54. Cf. Bernard Capelle, "Autorité de la liturgie chez les Pères," *Recherches de Théologie ancienne et médiévale, 21* (1954), 5–22.

the next centuries and was to be quoted in the decrees of both the Council of Ephesus and the Council of Chalcedon.[55] It seems to have been called forth by the recrudescence, after the defeat of Arianism, of the ancient Docetic heresy, which denied the true and full humanity of Jesus or claimed that he did not have a genuinely human body.[56] Some were even going so far as to maintain that the body of Christ was of one essence [*homoousion*] with the Logos.[57] This new species of Docetism, about whose teachings scholars are still not agreed, is often seen as a forerunner of the Apollinarist theology.

In his response Athanasius argued on the basis of "the divine Scriptures" and of the decrees of "the fathers assembled at Nicaea" and accused the neo-Docetists of having outdone even the Arians. "You have gone further in impiety than any heresy. For if the Logos is of one essence with the body, the commemoration and the office of Mary are superfluous [*perittē tēs Marias hē mnēmē kai hē chreia*]."[58] And in his epistle to Maximus, combating the doctrine that the Logos had become man as a necessary consequence of his nature, Athanasius declared again: "If this were so, the commemoration [*mnēmē*] of Mary would be superfluous."[59] The theological point Athanasius was making seems quite clear: Mary was again, as she had been

55. Cf. George Ludwig, *Athanasii epistula ad Epictetum* (Jena, 1911), a careful textual analysis; on the role of the epistle to Epictetus at Ephesus and Chalcedon, see pp. 22–25. Ludwig's textual observations are supplemented by Opitz, pp. 173–74.

56. Cf. Grillmeier, pp. 204–05, 214–17, on the significance of the *Epistola ad Epictetum.*

57. Athanasius, *Epistola ad Epictetum* 9, PG 26, 1064.

58. Ibid. 4, PG 26, 1056–57.

59. Athanasius, *Epistola ad Maximum philosophum* 3, PG 26, 1088.

to the anti-Gnostic fathers,[60] the guarantee of the true humanity of Jesus Christ.

What is not so clear is the precise character of the *mnēmē* to which Athanasius was referring. If the word meant no more than "memory," as it did in the New Testament and elsewhere,[61] then he would have been arguing that the remembrance of Mary, as enshrined for example in the creed or in memorial prayers, necessarily implied that the humanity of Christ took its beginning from her and had not preexisted from eternity. But *mnēmē* sometimes had a technical significance in the formation of the Christian calendar, referring to the anniversary of a saint.[62] Martin Jugie, in his early study of the first festivals devoted to Mary in both the East and the West, contended that the *mnēmē* of Mary referred to in early fifth-century documents was not the anniversary of her death or "dormition" [*koimēsis*], but of her "nativity," which may have meant her entry into heaven.[63] In his later and massive study of

60. Cf. Th. Camelot, "Introduction" to Ignace d'Antioche, *Lettres*, Sources chrétiennes *10* (Paris, 1958), 26–29, and the passages from Ignatius cited there.

61. Thus in 2 Peter 1:15, *tēn toutōn mnēmēn poieisthai* is translated "to recall these things."

62. Cf. Basil, *Epistolae* xciii, *PG 32*, 484, *mnēmē hagiou* [or, in a variant reading, *martyros*] *tinos*, "the feast-day of some saint [or martyr]." The choice between the two textual variants is relevant to our question, for some scholars have argued for *martyros* on the grounds that only martyrs were commemorated at Basil's time. The earliest reference to an annual memorial appears to be in *Martyrium Polycarpi* xviii, where *mnēmē* is used but apparently not in the technical heortological sense; see William R. Schoedel, ed., *Polycarp, Martyrdom of Polycarp, Fragments of Papias*, Vol. 5 of Robert M. Grant, ed., *The Apostolic Fathers: A New Translation and Commentary* (New York, 1967), pp. 75–76.

63. Martin Jugie, "La première fete mariale en Orient et en Occident. L'Avent primitif," *Echos d'Orient, 22* (1923), 129–52.

the death and assumption of the Virgin he repeated, corrected, and amplified this argument.[64] For our purposes, however, this problem is secondary to the fundamental one. Is *tēs Marias hē mnēmē* a reference to some mariological festival? There is some evidence to support the existence of a festival called the *mnēmē* of Mary and celebrated on the Sunday before Christmas,[65] but the evidence does not go back quite as far as Athanasius. Nevertheless, both that evidence and his language seem to make it plausible that such a commemoration of Mary was being kept already during his time and that his argument was based upon it.

He would then have been arguing that there was no justification for a festival commemorating the Virgin Mary the *Theotokos* if she had not played a part in the salvation of man. She belonged to the New Testament, not to the Old, and was not remembered, as the saints of ancient Israel were, as a prophet of the coming of Christ. Rather, she had a function or office, a *chreia*, as the chosen and commissioned instrument through whom the uncreated Logos received his created humanity. And that *chreia* or ministry was celebrated with grateful remembrance in the observance of the *mnēmē* or commemoration of Mary.

The *chreia* was a given fact of the history of salvation; the *mnēmē* was a given fact of Christian observance. Both the creed of the Church and the calendar of the Church, then, attested the doctrine that the human nature of Christ was a creature, just as they attested the doctrine that the divine nature of Christ was not a creature; and the sign of the bond between Christ the creature and mankind the creature was "the commemoration and the office of Mary,"

64. Jugie, *La mort et l'Assomption de la Sainte Vierge,* esp. pp. 172–212.
65. See the brief but informative discussion in Graef, pp. 133–38.

which would be superfluous if the humanity of Christ were some sort of component of his preexistence as the Logos of God. Although it is undeniable, from the evidence, that Athanasius never worked out as satisfactory a formula for the implications of the full and true humanity of the Lord as he did for those of his deity, it is equally clear that both aspects of the "double account"[66] were vouched for by the authority of the orthodox faith.

In the composition and identification of that authority, the worship and devotion of the Church were seen as an important constituent element of the definition of what Athanasius, in the conclusion of the epistle to Epictetus, called "the confession of that faith which is both devout and orthodox."[67] If Mary was *Theotokos,* as the language of Christian devotion declared she was, the relation between the divine and human in Jesus Christ had to be such as to justify this apparently incongruous term; hence the doctrine of the "communication of the properties." If Mary had the "office" of clothing the Logos in an authentic and therefore created humanity, as in the "commemoration of Mary" the practice of Christian devotion declared she had, no aversion to flesh and blood could be permitted to vitiate the doctrine of the incarnation. To qualify as a dogma of the Church, then, a doctrine had to conform not only to the apostolic tradition, as set down in Scripture and in such magisterial witnesses as the decrees of the Council of Nicaea, but also to the worship and devotion of the Church Catholic.

The mutual concordance of devotion and dogma in the mariology of Athanasius deserves consideration as another

66. Athanasius, *Oratio III. contra Arianos* 29, PG 26, 385.
67. *Hē homologia tēs eusebous kai orthodoxou pisteōs:* Athanasius, *Epistola ad Epictetum* 12, PG 26, 1069.

principle and method of the development of doctrine. This is not to claim that Athanasius was operating with a systematic theory about this congruence, but his coupling of *mnēmē* with *chreia* or of *eusebeia* with *orthodoxia* would suggest that proper praying and proper teaching together made the Church orthodox.[68] He devoted his life to the defense of the Council of Nicaea against all its enemies, foreign and domestic; in the *Letter to the Virgins* discussed earlier, he appears to have introduced references to its decrees with the formula "it is written," usually used to introduce proof texts from the Bible.[69] But for the development of the doctrine of Mary that, according to Athanasius, was implied in the decrees of Nicaea, the lead had been taken by the devotional and liturgical development of the Church, which in its ascription of the title *Theotokos* to the Virgin Mary had anticipated the formal conciliar promulgation of the doctrine by more than a century.

It is, to be sure, far easier to assert the legitimacy of this method of doctrinal development than it is to specify its limits. Thus Newman, in his essay *On Consulting the Faithful in Matters of Doctrine,* formulated the positive thesis: "In most cases when a definition [of doctrine] is contemplated, the laity will have a testimony to give; but if ever there be an instance when they ought to be consulted, it is

---

68. The same linking of *eusebeia* and *orthodoxia* with *thrēskeia* (liturgical observance) occurs as early as the second half of the third century; cf. Methodius of Olympus, *Symposium* viii.10, *PG 18, 153.* In Byzantium, of course, the Feast of Orthodoxy *(hē kyriakē tēs orthodoxias)* came to be celebrated on the first Sunday of Lent in commemoration of a liturgical milestone, the restoration of the icons by the Empress Theodora.

69. Athanasius, *Lettre aux Vierges, CSCO* 150, 77–78 (Coptic); 151, 59 (French), and Lefort's n. 27 there on the *Gnomes du concile de Nicée* attributed to Athanasius.

in the case of doctrines which bear directly upon devotional sentiments."[70] But even he went on to warn that a loss of the concordance between devotion and doctrine "will terminate . . . in superstition" among simple believers.[71] The dogma of the assumption of Mary is probably the most striking example of how the elevation of devotion to the status of doctrine can call forth controversy about development of doctrine; even the dogma's defenders will admit that there are forms of devotion to Mary that do not deserve such elevation.[72] Within the context of the present discussion of the mariology of Athanasius, however, it is necessary only to take account of his reliance on devotion and liturgy to prove the "double account" that Mary the creature was the Mother of God and that her Son also was, on his human side, a creature.

SPECIFYING THE SUBJECT

The creaturely status of Mary in relation to Christ indicates yet another line of development which doctrine sometimes seems to take, namely, the task of specifying more accurately the proper subject for predicates that have been misplaced by heresy. Most of the controversies in the fourth century dealt with the propriety of predications such as *homoousios* or *Theotokos*. But the literature of the controversies also suggests, or at least hints at, a definition of heresy as misplaced predication, to which the eventual orthodox answer was the specification of the subject. Only at the Council of Ephesus and beyond was this answer supplied,

70. John Henry Newman, *On Consulting the Faithful in Matters of Doctrine* (Coulson ed.), p. 104.

71. Ibid., p. 106.

72. Cf. Rahner, "Virginitas in partu," *Schriften zur Theologie, 4,* 173–205.

but by hindsight we may see an earlier stage of the development in the Arian controversy.

The Arian heresy, in the words of Henry M. Gwatkin,
"degraded the Lord of Saints to the level of his creatures."[73]
What it ascribed to Christ was more than it was willing to
ascribe to any of the saints, but less than it ascribed to the
supreme deity. The Arian doctrine concerning the saints
is not easy to assemble from the fragments, though we know
that the *Thalia* of Arius spoke of "the elect of God, the wise
men of God, his holy sons."[74] There is some evidence that
certain legends of the saints have come down through Arian
sources.[75] We are considerably better informed about the
Arian view of the relation between Christ and the saints.
According to the letter of the Arians to Alexander, the
Logos was a "perfect creature of God, but not as one of the
creatures,"[76] since he was the creature through whom God
had made all the other creatures; therefore the "superiority"
of this creature over all the other creatures was that he was
created directly while they were created through him.[77]

In his preexistence, then, the Logos was the perfect creature. But in his earthly career he became the perfect creature. Arianism seems in its picture of the man Jesus Christ
to have combined a denial of the presence of a human soul
in him[78] with the Samosatenian doctrine that he made himself worthy of elevation to the status of "Son of God" by

73. Henry Melville Gwatkin, *Studies of Arianism* (Cambridge, 1882), p. 265.
74. Quoted in Athanasius, *Oratio I. contra Arianos* 5, PG 26, 20.
75. Cf. Gwatkin, pp. 134–35, n. 3.
76. Quoted in Athanasius, *De synodis* 16, PG 26, 709.
77. Athanasius, *De decretis Nicaenae synodi* 9, PG 25, 432.
78. But see William P. Haugaard, "Arius: Twice a Heretic? Arius and the
Human Soul of Jesus Christ," *Church History, 29* (1960), 251–63.

his "moral progress."[79] The Arians are reputed to have taught that God had elected him "because of his foreknowledge" that Christ would not rebel against him, but would, "by his care and self-discipline [*dia epimeleian kai askēsin*]," triumph over his "mutable nature" and remain faithful.[80] Because the sonship of the Logos was a function of his perfect creaturehood and the sonship of the man Jesus was a consequence of his perfect obedience, the difference between his sonship and that of the saints was quantitative rather than qualitative, for by their own perfect obedience they could eventually attain to a participation in the same sonship.

Now this Arian doctrine of participation by the saints in the sonship of Christ had a counterpart in the orthodox Athanasian doctrine of participation through "divinization": "Because of our relationship to his body we, too, have become God's temple, and in consequence are made God's sons, in such a way that even in us the Lord is now being worshiped."[81] The sonship was due not to imitation by the saints but to transformation by Christ, who, in the famous Athanasian formula, became human in order that the saints might become divine.[82] Athanasius contended that such a transformation and divinization was possible only because the Logos was Creator rather than creature. The Savior could mediate between God and humanity only because he himself was God. He was not promoted to a new status because he was the greatest of the saints, but

79. The Greek word was *prokopē;* cf. Athanasius, *De synodis* 26, *PG 26,* 729. See also n. 85 below.

80. Quoted in Theodoret, *Historia Ecclesiastica* i.12–13, *GCS 44,* 11.

81. Athanasius, *Oratio I. contra Arianos* 43, *PG 26,* 100.

82. Athanasius, *Oratio de incarnatione Verbi* 54, *PG 25,* 192; cf. Pelikan, *The Light of the World,* p. 120, ns. 18–21, and the literature cited there.

was restored to his eternal status. Now the saints became sons of God, creatures in whom the Creator dwelt so fully that he could be worshiped in them. That is what Arianism tried to make of Christ, a creature in whom the Creator dwelt so fully that God could be worshiped in him, the highest of the saints and therefore the mediator between God and man.

Mediation—Created and Uncreated

By drawing the line between Creator and creature and confessing that the Son of God belonged on God's side of that line, Nicene orthodoxy made possible and necessary a qualitative distinction between him and even the highest of the saints, between his uncreated mediation and their created mediation.[83] Now that the subject of the Arian sentences was changed, what was to become of all the predicates? What we have seen so far in the mariology of Athanasius would seem to indicate that, in a sense quite different from that implied by Harnack, "what the Arians had taught about Christ, the orthodox now taught about Mary,"[84] so that these creaturely predicates did not belong to Jesus Christ, the Son of God, but to the Virgin Mary, the Mother of God.

The portrait of Mary in the *Letter to the Virgins* of Athanasius would fit the Arian description of the Son of God, who "was chosen because, though mutable by nature, his painstaking character suffered no deterioration." Athanasius spoke of her "progressing" and may even have used

83. Newman, *Essay,* pp. 404–06, contains certain suggestions of this line of development.
84. Harnack, *Lehrbuch der Dogmengeschichte,* 2, 477.

the word *prokopē*, "moral progress," which the Arians had used of Christ.[85] Her progress, according to Athanasius, involved struggles with doubts and evil thoughts, but she triumphed over them and could thus become "the image" and "the model" of virginity for all those who strove for perfection, in short, the highest of the saints. Thus the first line of development we have traced here, evidenced by the *Letter to the Virgins*, seems to have led in this direction. So does the second line of development, for the devotional language *(Theotokos)* and the devotional practice *(mnēmē)* that lie behind the mariology of Athanasius are the prime instance in all his thought of the doctrine that even a creature could become deserving of worship by virtue of the indwelling of the Creator. The hymn from which Athanasius may have been quoting the title *Theotokos*, the Greek original of *Sub tuum presidium*, was likewise the prime instance of such worship.[86]

It remained for further controversy to call forth further clarification of the doctrine, but in the light of that controversy we may see already in Athanasius that it was a development by the specification of the subject. When the development did come, it came first and most fully in the Greek-speaking East, where, as we have seen, the ascetical and the devotional presuppositions of the doctrine of Mary were present long before they appeared in the West. Causes and influences are notoriously elusive, and both historians and theologians have often been more informed about them

85. The Coptic translation reads *esprokopte*, suggesting that the Greek original had *prokopē* or some cognate: Athanasius, *Lettre aux Vierges, CSCO* 150, 78 (Coptic); 151, 60 (French). On *prokopē*, cf. n. 79 above.

86. Maurice Gordillo, *Mariologia Orientalis* (Rome, 1954), pp. 7–8, n. 56; G. Meersseman, *Der Hymnos Akathistos im Abendland, 1* (Freiburg Schweiz, 1958), 14–15.

than they have had a right to be. But it does seem plausible that Athanasius could help to shape the development of the doctrine of Mary at least partly because these two sets of presuppositions were present, just as he made further development of the doctrine possible by his defense of the Nicene distinction.

Far from "beclouding" the West with "the darkness of their smooth talk" or "confusing Latin purity with Greek confusion," the Greek fathers made a significant contribution to the development of the doctrine of Mary in the West. To no doctrine did Newman recur oftener in the *Essay on Development* than to this one. It was, together with its corollaries such as the virgin life and the cultus of the saints and the angels, the chief issue in the fourth test, "Early Anticipation";[87] it took up more than half of the discussion in support of the sixth test, "Conservative Action on its Past."[88] Writing a decade before the promulgation of the dogma of the immaculate conception by Pope Pius IX in *Ineffabilis Deus* of December 8, 1854, Newman knew that mariological doctrine had to be the crucial test case for any theory of a continuing doctrinal development.[89] When that dogma was promulgated, he had to return to the issue,[90] but the view represented by his *Essay on Development* was substantially unchanged. As Newman himself said, however, "whether the minute facts of history will bear me out in this view, I leave to others to determine."[91]

87. Newman, *Essay*, pp. 384–87.

88. Ibid., pp. 435–45.

89. See Günter Biemer, *Newman on Tradition,* trans. Kevin Smyth (New York, 1967), pp. 107–08, n. 84.

90. Newman, *On Consulting the Faithful* (Coulson ed.), p. 104.

91. Cf. Aubrey Gwynn, "Newman and the Catholic Historian" in Michael Tierney, ed., *A Tribute to Newman* (Dublin, 1945), p. 284.

5
Hilary on Filioque

Many of the ideas stated in the *Essay on Development* appeared at an earlier stage of their own development in a sermon Newman delivered on February 2, 1843, based on Luke 2:19. Printed versions of the *University Sermons* entitle the sermon "The Theory of Developments in Religious Doctrine,"[1] and in it Newman declared:

> Again, the doctrine of the Double Procession was no Catholic dogma in the first ages, though it was more or less clearly stated by individual Fathers; yet, if it is now to be received, as surely it must be, as part of the Creed, it was really held everywhere from the beginning, and therefore, in a measure, held as a mere religious impression, and perhaps an unconscious one.[2]

DEVELOPMENT OF THE DOCTRINE OF THE HOLY SPIRIT

This amazing sentence, which Owen Chadwick has called "one of those frustrating passages which from time to time baffle and trouble every reader of Newman,"[3] sets forth the most graphic illustration in the history of the relations be-

1. See Louis Bouyer, *Newman: His Life and Spirituality*, trans. J. Lewis May (New York, 1960), pp. 225–27, for an evaluation of this sermon.
2. John Henry Newman, *Sermons, Chiefly on the Theory of Religious Belief, Preached before the University of Oxford* (1st ed. London, 1843), p. 324.
3. Chadwick, *From Bossuet to Newman*, p. 235.

tween Eastern and Western Christendom of the connection between doctrinal development and Christian unity,
namely, the question of whether in the internal relations
of the Trinity the Holy Spirit proceeds only from the
Father, as the Greeks contended, or from the Father and
the Son, "ex patre Filioque," as the Latins argued.

The history of the dogma of the Holy Spirit has been,
until modern mariological doctrine, the classic illustration
of the entire problem of doctrinal development. The evolution of this dogma called forth from the fourth-century
Greek theologian, Gregory of Nazianzus, the following explanation, which has been called "a highly original theory
of doctrinal development":[4] "The Old Testament proclaimed the Father manifestly, and the Son more hiddenly.
The New [Testament] manifested the Son, and suggested
the deity of the Spirit. Now the Spirit himself is resident
among us, and provides us with a clearer explanation of
himself."[5] Thomas Aquinas, too, felt constrained to pro-
pound his theory of doctrinal development, in his exposition of the doctrine of the Holy Spirit and in defense of the
Filioque. When a church council appeared to have gone
beyond its predecessors, Thomas argued, this was not to be
interpreted as the promulgation of a "new creed," but as
the clarification and making explicit of what had already
been implied in the earlier formulation. Therefore, according to Thomas, "the truth [of the Filioque] was contained implicitly in the faith that the Holy Spirit proceeds
from the Father."[6] The Greek father and the Latin doctor
were thus agreed that the doctrine of the Holy Spirit raises

4. Kelly, *Early Christian Doctrines*, p. 261.
5. Gregory of Nazianzus, *Orationes* xxxi.26, *PG 36*, 161.
6. Thomas Aquinas, *Summa Theologica* i.36.3, *Opera, 1*, 148.

the question of doctrinal development in a very arresting form.

By common consent of both his Latin admirers and his Greek detractors,[7] Augustine was the theologian whose trinitarian speculations in his *On the Trinity* formulated the Filioque for Latin theology:

> Nor can we say that the Holy Spirit does not proceed also from the Son, for it is not without purpose that the same Spirit is said to be the Spirit both of the Father and of the Son. . . . [John 20:22 is a demonstration that] the Holy Spirit proceeds not only from the Father, but also from the Son.[8]

Ironically, it was in this treatise more than almost anywhere else that Augustine wanted to act as an expositor not of his private religious reflections or theological speculations, but of the faith of the Church. In the introduction to the treatise he declared, after summarizing the trinitarian doctrine of both Eastern and Western orthodoxy: "This is also my faith, inasmuch as this is the Catholic faith,"[9] or, as he termed it at the end of Book I, "the right faith of the Catholic Church."[10]

Recent research, especially an enlightening series of articles by Berthold Altaner, has examined in detail Augustine's debt to the dogmatic and exegetical tradition of the

7. Cf. Martin Jugie, *De processione Spiritus Sancti: ex fontibus revelationis et secundum Orientales dissidentes* (Rome, 1936), pp. 202–09; and Cyril C. Richardson, "The Enigma of the Trinity" in Roy W. Battenhouse, ed., *A Companion to the Study of St. Augustine* (New York, 1955), p. 245.

8. Augustine, *De Trinitate* iv.29, *PL 42*, 908.

9. Ibid. i.7, *PL 42*, 824.

10. Ibid. i.31, *PL 42*, 844.

Greek fathers.[11] Even though his use of the Latin tradition
has not received similar attention, the very paucity of explicit citations from the fathers in the *On the Trinity*—by
comparison, for example, with the arguments over Cyprian
in the controversies with Pelagianism and Donatism[12]—
suggests that in his explanation of the dogma of the Trinity,
Augustine believed himself to be a spokesman for the orthodox consensus of the fathers, both Greek and Latin, insofar
as he was able to read them.[13]

THE IMPORTANCE OF HILARY

Most scholars would agree that Augustine's chief source
of information about this orthodox consensus was Hilary
of Poitiers, who between 356 and 360 had written a treatise
On the Faith, which eventually came to be called *On the
Trinity.*[14] Hilary was, in any event, the only ecclesiastical
writer quoted by name in Augustine's *On the Trinity,* and
lauded as "a man of no mediocre authority in treating the
Scriptures and in asserting the faith."[15] Alfred Schindler
has suggested that both the quotation from Hilary itself and
the context in which Augustine used it make it seem un-
likely that Augustine had Hilary's book before him when

11. These have now been collected in Berthold Altaner, *Kleine patristische
Schriften,* esp. pp. 181–331.

12. See pp. 66–67, 76–79 above.

13. Cf. Augustine, *De Trinitate* iii.Pr.1, *PL 42,* 867–69, on Augustine's
ability to read the Greek fathers; also Altaner, pp. 129–53: "Augustinus und
die griechische Sprache."

14. On the title, see the recent study of C. F. A. Borchardt, *Hilary of
Poitier's Role in the Arian Struggle,* Kerkhistorische Studien (The Hague,
1966), pp. 39–40; on the theology, cf. also P. Smulders, *La doctrine trinitaire
de S. Hilaire de Poitiers,* Analecta Gregoriana (Rome, 1944).

15. Augustine, *De Trinitate* vi.11, *PL 42,* 931.

he wrote. Schindler finds it possible to say that "Hilary's influence does not go very deep and disappears especially at the point where Augustine goes beyond the mere proof of the dogma from Scripture."[16] This remark illustrates one of the chief weaknesses in most studies of the development of the doctrine of the Trinity, and therefore of the Filioque: a lack of attention to "the mere proof of the dogma from Scripture" in patristic writers, who themselves regarded such proof as anything but "mere." Yet there continues to appear one truncated edition and translation of Augustine's *On the Trinity* after another, in which the biblical argumentation of the first half of the treatise is eliminated or summarized with a few cavalier remarks, while the discussion of the natural analogies to the Trinity in the second half receives all the space.[17] At the very least, this is a reversal of the theological priorities as Augustine saw them.

This overemphasis on the trinitarian analogies both in the editions and in secondary works has obscured many of the lines of development in the history of the doctrine of the Trinity, lines which will not become clear until scholars have investigated and described the specific course of the exegesis of crucial passages from Scripture, especially from the Old Testament. Thus Hilary may not be an important source for Augustine's notion of the "vestiges of the Trinity," but only a study of Hilary's trinitarian interpretation of Scripture in comparison with that of Ambrose and

16. Alfred Schindler, *Wort und Analogie in Augustins Trinitätslehre,* p. 129.

17. To cite only two instances: Whitney J. Oates, ed., *Basic Writings of Saint Augustine* (2 vols. New York, 1948), 2, 667–878; and John Burnaby, ed., *Augustine: Later Works,* The Library of Christian Classics (Philadelphia, 1955), pp. 37–181, where the biblical argument of Books I–IV is summarized in one page, pp. 19–20.

of the Greek fathers will make it possible to assess his significance for Augustine's thought about the doctrine of the Trinity and thus for the development of that doctrine in the Latin West.[18] Otherwise, the problem of doctrinal development cannot be examined historically. Because the history of doctrinal development has not always followed the course which common sense or theological logic prescribes for it a priori, only the careful *explication de texte* provides a reliable basis for speaking about the course of the development of a doctrine.

Common sense and theological logic both would seem to prescribe, for example, that the Filioque should proceed as a corollary from the dogma of the personhood, the deity, and the coequality of the Holy Spirit with the Father and the Son in the Trinity. If the Holy Spirit is truly God and a divine person in the same sense as the Father and the Son, does he proceed from the Father only or from the Father and the Son? That is the order in which the questions are considered in the textbooks of dogma issued by those churches in which this is still a real issue.[19] But that is not quite the order in which the doctrines themselves developed, or at least not the order in which they were developed by Augustine's mentor, Hilary of Poitiers.

In some ways it is easier to discover Hilary's thought about the Filioque than to discern his position on the deity of the Holy Spirit. As Erasmus, among others, noted,[20] Hilary was extremely chary about specifying the place of

18. See the article by Löffler referred to in p. 6, n. 6 above.

19. Cf., for instance, Charles Hodge, *Systematic Theology, 1* (New York, 1872), 477–78, 522–34.

20. *Opus Epistolarum Des. Erasmi,* ed. P. S. Allen (Oxford, 1906 ff.), *5,* 1334, p. 180.

the Holy Spirit in the Trinity; and even in the conclusion of his *On the Trinity* he would only say: "I will say nothing about thy Holy Spirit except that he is thy Spirit."[21] Repeatedly he seemed to speak of the divine element in Christ as "Spirit" or even as "Holy Spirit,"[22] thus giving the occasion for some historians to attribute "binitarianism" to him,[23] and for his orthodox interpreters to feel obliged to defend him against the charge of heresy in his doctrine, if not of confusion in his thought. On the other hand, as scholars have long recognized, Hilary asserted a position very much like the Western doctrine of the Filioque: "He [the Holy Spirit] receives from the Son; he is also sent by [the Son] and proceeds from the Father. I ask whether to receive from the Son is the same as to proceed from the Father." The answer was that in any event "to receive from the Son is the same as to receive from the Father."[24] He went on to show that, in biblical language, the Holy Spirit did receive both from the Father and from the Son. Therefore an earlier passage, referring to the Holy Spirit as one "qui [a] Patre et Filio auctoribus, confitendus est,"[25] probably does mean, as one translator has rendered it: "We are bound to confess Him [the Holy Spirit], proceeding, as He does, from Father and Son."[26] And only the doctrine of the

---

21. Hilary, *De Trinitate* xii.56, *PL 10,* 471.

22. "Spiritum sanctum hic Verbum ipsum intelligi manifestum est": editor's note to Hilary, *De Trinitate* ii.24, *PL 10,* 66.

23. Cf. Friedrich Loofs, *Leitfaden zum Studium der Dogmengeschichte* (6th ed. Tübingen, 1959), p. 200, n. 3, and p. 122, n. 14.

24. Hilary, *De Trinitate* viii.20, *PL 10,* 251.

25. Ibid. ii.29, *PL 10,* 69; on the textual variants see n. (a) there.

26. E. W. Watson et al., trans., *St. Hilary of Poitiers. Select Works,* A Select Library of Nicene and Post-Nicene Fathers, Second Series, *9* (New York, 1899), 60, and Watson's note.

Filioque can make sense of the theology in Books II and VIII of Hilary's *On the Trinity*.[27]

HESITANCY ABOUT SPECULATION

Evidently Hilary did not first have to substantiate the full deity and the personhood of the Holy Spirit and then speculate his way to a Filioque doctrine, illumined in his thinking by the contemplation of the vestiges of the Trinity in the world and in the human soul. No characteristic of Hilary's thought is more evident than his hesitancy about theological speculation, which became particularly acute when he came to discuss the doctrine of the Holy Spirit. He would have preferred to say nothing more than Scripture itself expressly said, but felt constrained to break his silence because of the attacks of heretics.[28] Over and over in the course of his treatise he quoted the words of Colossians 2:8, "See to it that no one makes a prey of you by philosophy and empty deceit," using them to warn his readers against speculative heresy.[29] So profound was the divine mystery that one could not "express it in words or determine it by reason or even embrace it by thought."[30] He had to admit that the attributes of the Father were easier to feel than to express.[31] All predications about the relation between the Father and the Son were inadequate, for both the generation of the Son and his being passed human understanding,

27. Hilary, *De Trinitate* ii.29–35, *PL 10*, 69–75; viii.19–32, *PL 10*, 250–61.

28. Ibid. ii.29, *PL 10*, 69.

29. Ibid. i.13, *PL 10*, 34; viii.53, *PL 10*, 276; ix.1, *PL 10*, 280; ix.8, *PL 10*, 287; xii.20, *PL 10*, 445.

30. Ibid. x.53, *PL 10*, 385. On the entire subject, cf. J. E. Emmenegger, *The Functions of Faith and Reason in the Theology of Saint Hilary of Poitiers* (Washington, 1947).

31. Hilary, *De Trinitate* ii.7, *PL 10*, 56.

as did everything else about God.[32] For Hilary, the proper alternative to speculation as a way of understanding God was worship.[33] The inadequacies of language made every confession unsatisfactory. The reality and the greatness of God transcended any formula. And therefore, God was "to be believed, to be apprehended, to be adored." Only by means of these duties of reverence could his true nature be expressed.[34]

Because of this inherent suspicion of speculation, Hilary was also highly sensitive to the inadequacy of any vestiges of the Trinity or other analogies between the Creator and the creature. Any such analogy was "useful for man" rather than "appropriate for God," for it provided adequate rather than complete information about the divine mystery.[35] Hilary used the familiar picture of the ladder to explain the function of these analogies in raising the human mind from the things of earth to the attainment of the true knowledge of God.[36] The metaphor of the Son of God as "light of light" in the Nicene Creed[37] could be understood in either a heretical or an orthodox way and therefore was not to be pressed beyond the point of comparison.[38] Similarly, the image of human birth could be used for the generation of the Son of God from his Father, but only within the proper limits, for it was an imperfect analogy.[39]

32. "Qui ultra sensum est, in nullo subjacet sensui": ibid. xii.31, *PL 10*, 452.

33. Ibid. xi.44, *PL 10*, 428.

34. Ibid. ii.7, *PL 10*, 57.

35. Ibid. i.19, *PL 10*, 38.

36. The Latin word he used was *gradus:* ibid. vi.9, *PL 10*, 163.

37. See p. 28, n. 50.

38. Hilary, *De Trinitate*, vi.12, *PL 10*, 165–67.

39. Ibid. vii.28, *PL 10*, 224.

Just as some heretics misapplied such analogies or pressed them beyond the proper point of comparison, so others claimed to have no need of any analogies to understand the mystery of the Godhead.

The theological method of Hilary was an effort to avoid both extremes. It was "heretical madness" to object to the orthodox doctrine on the grounds that it employed physical analogies for the divine nature. On the contrary, such analogies were altogether proper and necessary, if one wanted "to believe God as he testifies about himself." This did not mean that there would be a perfect correspondence between God the Creator and the creature used as a "physical comparison." But it did mean that God was not to be accused of having lied to men through the use of such a comparison. For although God was spirit, as John 4:24 taught, and man was flesh born of flesh, as John 3:6 taught, the spiritual reality of God could not be grasped except through the use of images taken from the world of flesh and of sense.[40]

Biblical Positivism

Hilary's reference to the use of such images by "God as he testifies about himself" was decisive in his argument, for he seems to have made use only of such analogies for the relation between persons in the Trinity as were used in the Scriptures themselves. These analogies were both necessary and dangerous, both legitimate and limited; but Hilary's twofold theological task, as an expositor of the Bible and as a defender of the Catholic faith, required him to probe the analogies for their orthodox meaning. Thus the funda-

40. Ibid. vii.30, *PL 10*, 225.

mental feature of Hilary's theological method was his bibli-
cism. A theology may be called biblicistic if it not only
begins with the words and events of the Bible, but single-
mindedly confines itself to them, even in the face of heretical provocation or orthodox speculation. And where the
words and events in the Bible are less than satisfying in the
data they provide—as they are, for example, in the doctrine
of the Holy Spirit—a biblical positivism such as Hilary's
will often be less than satisfying as well.

And so, according to Hilary, "the spoken language of
God [*Dei sermo*]" was the only proper way for a man to
speak about God; if he used "other words" than those which
had come from God himself, he would either misunderstand
the things of God or cause his readers to do so.[41] Near the
end of *On the Trinity,* he identified "the sayings of the
apostolic and prophetic proclamation" as the boundaries
within which Christian confession, and therefore Christian
theology, were to be carried on.[42] Even the apostle Paul,
whose epistles were part of that "apostolic proclamation,"
had not spoken merely on his own apostolic authority, but
had substantiated his message by reference to the Scriptures
of the Old Testament, to make it clear that Christian confession dealt "not so much with the names of the things
themselves as with the dynamics of the Scriptures [*Scrip-
turarum virtutibus*]." Therefore the Pauline motto, "in
accordance with the Scriptures [*secundum Scripturas*],"
became a refrain in Hilary's argument.[43] With this motto
the apostle had pointed to the doctrines and even to the

41. Ibid. vii.38, *PL 10,* 231.

42. Ibid. xii.26, *PL 10,* 449, and n. (d) there.

43. Ibid. x.67, *PL 10,* 395, where *secundum Scripturas* is repeated eight
times.

language of the Scriptures as the only safe harbor in which there was protection against the adverse winds of dispute and speculation. "The private opinions of men" were to cease and to be silent, and "human counsels" were not to be permitted to extend themselves beyond what God himself had promulgated.[44] "God is to be believed when he speaks of himself [*Ipsi de se Deo credendum est*]": the theology of Hilary was a theology of the word of God, even and especially when he came to speak about the relation between Father, Son, and Holy Spirit in the Trinity. This may help to explain the relative infrequency of the term *Trinitas* in Hilary's writings.[45]

CONGRUENCE OF IMMANENT AND ECONOMIC

It also helps to explain why Hilary, who held back so steadfastly from inventing or even employing analogies from the created realm to explain the divine reality, was equally steadfast in positing and developing a congruence between the internal life of God and his acts in relation to the created realm, or, to use the common theological distinction, between the immanent and the economic Trinity.[46] That congruence was, in turn, one of the methodological errors to which Greek theologians attributed the Western idea of the Filioque. So, for example, Theophylact,

44. Ibid. iv.14, *PL 10,* 107.

45. It seems to appear in only two passages in the entire treatise, both of them in the first book: i.22, *PL 10,* 39; and i.36, *PL 10,* 48. As we have noted on p. 123, the original title of the book was probably *De Fide,* not *De Trinitate.*

46. Greek-speaking theologians distinguished between *theologia* and *oikonomia.* Cf., e.g. Eusebius, *Historia Ecclesiastica* i.I.7, *GCS 9,* Pt. I, 8; and my comments on this passage in *Finality,* p. 28.

a Bulgarian archbishop of the eleventh century, maintained that the Latins "suppose that proceeding [*ekporeuesthai*] is identical with being imparted [*chorēgeisthai*] and with being conferred [*metadidosthai*] because the Spirit is discovered to have been sent and imparted and conferred from the Son."[47] Charitably, he blamed this confusion on the well-known poverty of the Latin tongue.[48]

Even in its Christian form, Latin had not developed a terminology precise enough to allow the proper distinction between the immanent "proceeding" of the Holy Spirit, which was from the Father only, and his economic "being sent, imparted, conferred," which was indeed also from the Son. Hilary was also aware of the greater subtlety and precision of Greek in such specific matters as *pronomina,* by which he appears to have meant not pronouns but definite articles.[49] But it is interesting that in the very paragraph in which he made this comparison between Greek and Latin he went on to speak of the distinction and the congruence between the immanent and the economic in the Trinity: the Son "has his God in the economy [*in dispensatione*] because he is a servant, and his Father in the [intratrinitarian] brightness because he is God."[50]

Hilary's preoccupation with the *dispensatio* and his concentration on the very words and phrases of Scripture for the exposition of the relations between Father, Son, and

47. Theophylact of Achrida, *Liber de iis quorum Latini incusantur* 5, *PG 126,* 228–29; cf. Steven Runciman, *The Eastern Schism: A Study of the Papacy and the Eastern Churches During the XIth and XIIth Centuries* (Oxford, 1956), pp. 71–74.

48. Cicero had already referred to a similar complaint in *Oratio pro Caecina* xviii.51, as had Seneca, *Epistolae* lviii.

49. Hilary, *De Trinitate,* xi.17, *PL 10,* 411.

50. Ibid.

Holy Spirit took propositional form in his insistence that the key to the doctrine of the Trinity was Matthew 28:19: "baptizing them in the name of the Father and of the Son and of the Holy Spirit." Commenting on these words, he found contained in them the entire "mystery of human salvation [*sacramentum salutis humanae*]," specifically "the meaning of the words, the efficacy of the realities, the order of the relations, and the understanding of the [divine] nature."[51] The "mystery of human salvation" was the economy [*dispensatio*] of the incarnation and redemption; "the understanding of the [divine] nature" was the immanent and eternal relation within the Trinity. Hilary then went on to expound the meaning of the terms in this passage and their bearing on the controverted issues.[52]

Into this trinitarian faith Hilary had been baptized, as his closing prayer emphasized once more with its reference to the "creed of my regeneration."[53] The vindication of the correctness of orthodox trinitarian doctrine would, he hoped, show that "the mystery of our regeneration [sc., through baptism], the mystery of the Trinity is intact and undefiled."[54] Although the chapter headings in the Benedictine edition of Hilary are not his own composition, the one provided by the editors for the opening of Book II summarizes his position very well: "That the knowledge of the Trinity supplied in baptism is sufficient."[55]

51. Ibid. ii.1, *PL 10*, 50.

52. Ibid. ii.5, *PL 10*, 53–54.

53. Ibid. xii.57, *PL 10*, 472: cf. J. N. D. Kelly, *Early Christian Creeds* (London, 1952), pp. 258–59.

54. Hilary, *De Trinitate*, i.36, *PL 10*, 48.

55. *PL 10*, 50.

The Holy Spirit as "Gift"

It has been suggested that Hilary's concentration on the baptismal formula as the basis for the understanding of the Trinity led him to use the baptismal terms *donum* and *munus*, "gift," as technical titles for the person of the Holy Spirit and thus to contribute to the confusion in the doctrine of the Holy Spirit within Western theology.[56] It is essential to note that in Hilary's usage *donum* and *munus* referred both to the economic and to the immanent. The names Father, Son, and Holy Spirit were taken to mean Author, Only-Begotten, and Gift; and again, "infinity in the Eternal, likeness in the Image, enjoyment in the Gift."[57] Both these highly unusual paraphrases of the names of the Trinity, the latter of which drew the attention of Augustine,[58] displayed the congruence that Hilary saw between the economic and the immanent in the Trinity. Even titles whose primary significance was clearly sacramental, i.e. economic, could be applied to the eternal relations within the Godhead.

But if this application was proper, the Filioque seemed the necessary conclusion, as Theophylact observed. There is an intriguing correspondence, though by no means an identity, between Theophylact's term *metadidosthai* and Hilary's term *donum,* perhaps even between his *chorēgeisthai* and Hilary's *munus.* The activities and qualities of the Holy Spirit signified by all these Greek and Latin terms were, as Theophylact acknowledged, both from the

56. Georg Kretschmar, *Studien zur frühchristlichen Trinitätstheologie,* Beiträge zur historischen Theologie (Tübingen, 1956), pp. 131–32.

57. Hilary, *De Trinitate,* ii.1, *PL 10, 51.*

58. Augustine, *De Trinitate,* vi.11, *PL 42, 931–32.*

Father and from the Son.[59] Hilary also recognized that the economic *donum* and *munus* of the Holy Spirit had to be "ex Patre Filioque"; he seems to have concluded that the immanent *ekporeuesthai* of the Holy Spirit was as well.

Such a congruence of the immanent and the economic was evident also in Hilary's statements about the second person of the Trinity. The relation of the Son to the Father was "a matter of origin and not of adoption, of reality and not of name, of birth and not of creation."[60] In a lengthy passage Hilary discussed the uniqueness of that eternal "birth" of God from God.[61] But the very same verb was also proper for the temporal, historical nativity of Jesus Christ from the Virgin Mary. He was "a human being born of Mary."[62] Sometimes Hilary juxtaposed the two births, showing both their congruence and the distinction between them. In one and the same paragraph he stated that "his birth is the mystery that the Father and the Son exist in the unity of [their] nature," and spoke of "the mystery of the body of the man born of Mary."[63]

As Athanasius spoke of a "double account,"[64] so Hilary distinguished a "twofold manner of speaking"[65] in the language of Scripture about Christ, not only in the parallelism of such terms as "Son of God" and "son of man,"[66] but in passages of Scripture that spoke of both the immanent and the economic relation between the Son and the Father, as,

59. Theophylact, loc. cit.
60. Hilary, *De Trinitate,* iii.11, *PL 10,* 82.
61. Ibid. ii.20, *PL 10,* 63.
62. Cf. ibid. iii.10, *PL 10,* 81; vi.31, *PL 10,* 182; ix.36, *PL 10,* 308.
63. Ibid. vii.26, *PL 10,* 222.
64. See p. 106, n. 46.
65. Cf. Hilary, *De Trinitate,* ix.5, *PL 10,* 284; "utriusque generis sermo."
66. Thus, for example, ibid. i.16, *PL 10,* 36–37.

according to Hilary, the words of Christ in John 16:28 did: "I came from the Father and have come into the world." These words were to be understood "with the most absolute accuracy as a description of their relationship." "I came from the Father" described their eternal and immanent relationship, for only God himself could "come from" God and exist by virtue of being born from God. On the other hand, "I have come into the world" referred to the economic. "The latter takes place in the economy, the former in the [divine] nature." And it was important to observe that "coming from the Father" and "coming into the world" were not identical.[67] Nevertheless, they were congruent, both in the case of the second person of the Trinity, who was born both eternally and historically, and in the case of the third person, who was a gift both eternally and historically. Therefore the apostrophe with which Hilary's treatise closed mingled the immanent and the economic motions of the Holy Spirit as it praised him for transcending all finite limits and all finite understanding.[68]

TRINITARIAN RECIPROCITY

Where Scripture was apparently unclear, therefore, as it was on the eternal procession of the Holy Spirit, Hilary seems to have been unwilling to develop a doctrine on the basis of analogies in creation. He was quite willing, however, to develop it on the basis of parallels between the revealing action of God and the eternal being of God. But there is another basis for developing a doctrine that seems to have been at work in Hilary's formulation of the Filioque. This could be called the principle of trinitarian reci-

67. Ibid. vi.31, *PL 10*, 182–83.
68. Ibid. xii.56, *PL 10*, 470–71.

procity. Some scholars hold that underlying the positions of
the Greek East and the Latin West on the procession of the
Holy Spirit were two different conceptions of the unity of
the Godhead. Philip Sherrard has stated this thesis in a
provocative way:

> The Greeks . . . tended always to keep very much to the
> fore . . . the idea of a real distinction of Persons in the
> Trinity. . . . But the Latins displaced it by a teaching in
> which the dominant position was given to the notion of
> the entire simplicity and non-differentiation of the divine
> nature.[69]

In Hilary's pronouncements on the issue, we find that he
was compelled to clarify the oneness of God and the sim-
plicity of his being because of the attacks of the Arians on
the Nicene definition. The biblical basis for Hilary's discussion of the being of God was what John Courtney Murray
called "the towering text,"[70] the words from the burning
bush in Exodus 3:14: "I am that I am." The importance of
these words not only for Hilary but for so many other
Christian theologians, both Greek and Latin, suggests the
desirability of a thorough study of the use of this theophany
in Jewish and early Christian thought.[71] According to
Hilary, this disclosure of the divine nature had been not
only decisive doctrinally but crucial personally for his own
conversion to Christianity. It had showed him that "nothing
is more appropriate to God than being," and being infinite-

---

69. Philip Sherrard, *The Greek East and the Latin West* (London, 1959),
p. 67.

70. Murray, *The Problem of God*, p. 5.

71. Cf. Pelikan, *Luther the Expositor*, pp. 24–27.

ly.[72] Although the passage was also being employed by the Arians to support their contention that the title "God" could not properly be applied to the Son,[73] to Hilary it proved the very opposite; for the theophanies of the Old Testament, including this one, were acts of the Son of God, who in this passage spoke as "the God who is."[74] In an extended and closely argued application of Exodus 3:14 to the relation between the Father and the Son in the being of the Godhead, Hilary concluded that "it belongs to [the Son's] nature for the Father to exist eternally and for him to be his Son eternally, and eternity is signified by the phrase 'he who is.' " Therefore the existence of the Son, by its participation in the absolute being of God, was eternal.[75] That is, the Son possessed absolute and eternal being because his being was eternally derived from the being of the Father, and the divine reality existed in the Logos.[76]

The Principle of Coinherence

The distinctions of Father, Son, and Holy Spirit could not mean, therefore, a division within the Godhead, for "God is simple."[77] Even natural reason taught that "the names of the same natures do not coincide without their being one."[78] But the proof of the oneness between Father, Son, and Holy Spirit came from the language of Scripture itself, in such passages as "I and the Father are one" (John

72. Hilary, *De Trinitate*, i.5, *PL 10*, 28.
73. Ibid. iv.8, *PL 10*, 102.
74. Ibid. v.22, *PL 10*, 144.
75. Ibid. xii.25, *PL 10*, 448.
76. Ibid. vii.11, *PL 10*, 208.
77. Ibid. ix.72, *PL 10*, 338.
78. Ibid. viii.4, *PL 10*, 239.

10:30), which, Hilary argued, must denote a unity in being and not a mere unity in will.[79] Was the ground of that unity, according to Hilary, the person of the Father or the being of the Godhead? Hilary's language is, unfortunately, not entirely free of ambiguity on this question. There are places where he used the title "God" to mean the Father as distinct from the Son;[80] he could even say that when the Son was called "God" by the Father, this was on the basis of "the name of the power [of the Father] which cannot be born."[81]

But when the challenges of the Arians compelled him to deal with the subtlety of such a passage as "I in the Father, and the Father in me" (John 14:11),[82] he formulated, more precisely than it had even been formulated before, the trinitarian principle of coinherence or circumincession: "The one is from the other, and they both are one essence [*unum*]. The two are not one person [*unus*], but one is in the other, for that [essence] which is in both is the same." From this it followed that they were "in each other mutually [*in se invicem*]." And therefore "this unity, this power, this love are in the Son and the Father."[83] As G. L. Prestige has observed, "All this is finely put, and in language free from unnecessary technicalities. And it marks a new advance in that it presents the conception of the several Persons of the godhead 'containing' one another."[84]

79. Ibid. viii.5–10, *PL 10*, 240–43. Cf. T. E. Pollard, "The Exegesis of John X.30 in the Early Trinitarian Controversies," *New Testament Studies*, 3 (1957), 339–49.

80. For example, Hilary, *De Trinitate* vii.17, *PL 10*, 207–08.

81. Ibid. iv.37, *PL 10*, 123.

82. Ibid. iii.1–4, *PL 10*, 76–78.

83. Ibid. iii.4, *PL 10*, 78.

84. G. L. Prestige, *God in Patristic Thought* (London, 1956), p. 286; on the other hand, Schindler, p. 184, dismisses it as "quite rudimentary."

In answer to the question of whether the unity of the Godhead was in the person of the Father or in the being of God, Hilary's doctrine would seem to have been that it was in the latter. Commenting on John 14:6–11 at the end of Book VII, he warned against interpreting the unity as a "transfusion of the one into the other," asserting instead that it was a "unity of the same nature in both through generation and birth."[85] That unity was also at issue in the question of whether the Holy Spirit proceeded from the Father or from the Son. Hilary's answer, as we have seen, was that the Spirit "receives from the Son," that "he is sent by [the Son] and proceeds from the Father."[86] Hilary did not acknowledge any difference between receiving from the Son and proceeding from the Father; in addition, there was no difference between receiving from the Father and receiving from the Son. This latter was characteristic of the Holy Spirit, who received from both the Father and the Son.[87] Therefore both the unity of the divine being and the reciprocity of relations within that unity seem to have led Hilary to the conclusion that the Holy Spirit proceeded from the Father and from the Son.

This conclusion, in turn, formed part of the basis for the most explicit affirmation in Hilary's treatise that the Holy Spirit belonged on God's side of the line dividing the Creator from the creature. As the name "creature" was not proper for Christ, so "I shall not tolerate it for thy Holy Spirit either, who proceeds from thee and is sent through

85. Hilary, *De Trinitate*, vii.41, *PL 10*, 234.
86. Ibid. vii.20, *PL 10*, 251.
87. Ibid. ix.73, *PL 10*, 340.

him [the Son]."[88] As he who revealed God had to be God himself,[89] so he who searched the depths of God could not be alien to the divine nature but had to be God.[90] Most of the argument against the Arians had been devoted to proving that "creature" was not an appropriate term for the Son of God, despite such statements as Proverbs 8:22:[91] "The Lord created me at the beginning of his work, the first of his acts of old."[92] Hilary found it consistent when those who spoke this way about the Son of God also went on to classify the Spirit as a creature and thus to undermine the mystery of the divine unity.[93]

The eventual formulation of the doctrine of the Holy Spirit as coeternal and coequal with the Father and the Son came only a few years after the death of Hilary; and he, together with Athanasius and Basil in the East and Ambrose in the West, had done much to assure the victory of that doctrine.[94] The doctrine of the Filioque did not become an issue until much later. But at least in the case of Hilary, Filioque came first.

88. Ibid. xii.55, *PL 10,* 469.
89. See, for example, ibid. v.20, *PL 10,* 143.
90. Ibid. xii.55–56, *PL 10,* 468–70.
91. See p. 102, n. 31.
92. Hilary, *De Trinitate,* xii.1, *PL 10,* 434; cf. Borchardt, pp. 92–95.
93. Hilary, *De Trinitate,* ii.4, *PL 10,* 53.
94. Cf. Hermann Dörries, *De Spiritu Sancto. Der Beitrag des Basilius zum Abschluss des trinitarischen Dogmas* (Göttingen, 1956), pp. 121–62.

Conclusion

Like Newman's *Essay on Development*, from which its title is derived, this book is a tentative *Forschungsbericht*, a report on work in progress. It has sought to put the problem of doctrinal development into focus as first and foremost a problem for historical investigation. Together with the evolutionary hypothesis with which it manifests certain superficial affinities,[1] Newman's theory of development, despite its brilliance and daring, must be checked against the concrete data and revised or even rejected on the basis of them. Compared with the *Essay*, therefore, this volume does not come to any theological conclusions as definite as Newman's, much less to any ecclesiastical decisions as dramatic. Nevertheless, a few observations are in order.

"There is," René Wellek has said, "an inner logic in the evolution of ideas, a dialectic of concepts."[2] Christian doctrines are ideas and concepts, but they are more. Christian doctrine is what the Church believes, teaches, and confesses as it prays and suffers, serves and obeys, celebrates and awaits the coming of the kingdom of God. It is also an expression of the broken state of Christian faith and witness, the most patent illustration of the truth of the apostolic admission

1. For a critical examination of these affinities, see Chadwick, *From Bossuet to Newman,* pp. 96–119: "Newman and the Philosophy of Evolution."

2. René Wellek, *A History of Modern Criticism: 1750–1950* (New Haven, 1955 ff.), *1,* 8.

in 1 Corinthians 13:12: "Now we see in a mirror dimly . . . Now I know in part." The "inner logic" in the evolution of doctrine must be discerned, therefore, in the matrix of the total life of the Christian community.

Theologians are spokesmen for that community; they are not a kind of corporate pope. It was the sacramental life of the community, not the speculation of its theologians, that brought forth Cyprian's doctrine of original sin. Similarly, the religious life—both the life of Christian devotion and the structured life of monastic communities—was responsible for the evolution of the doctrine of Mary in the thought of Athanasius. By his emphasis on this communal matrix, Newman, both in the *Essay on Development* and in *On Consulting the Faithful in Matters of Doctrine*,[3] provided a much-needed corrective to the overemphasis of German Lutheran *Dogmengeschichte* on the great ideas of the great theologians—an overemphasis that has had as its almost unavoidable corollary a preoccupation with discontinuity.

But the presence of that overemphasis is no justification for a procrustean theory of development which proceeds on the assumption that doctrines would not dare to have developed in any other way. It must be admitted that here Newman's existential purpose did get in the way of his historical vision. For example, there was no logical reason for Hilary to develop the notion of the double procession before he had clarified the doctrine that appears to be its presupposition, the divinity and personhood of the Holy Spirit. The doctrinal heterogeneity both within and between various periods of church history is far less malleable

3. See the comments of John Coulson, "Introduction" to Newman, *On Consulting the Faithful*, pp. 23–27.

than Newman's slightly pat "tests . . . of varying cogency and independence"[4] would lead the historically unsophisticated to believe. Newman's reliance on organic metaphors to account for development, to which various of his critics have called attention,[5] precludes the kind of radical change that has occurred from time to time in the history of Christian doctrine. It also obscures a characteristic of dogma described by Hans Küng:

> Doctrinal statements of the Church are, even though they have the assistance of the Holy Spirit, *human* formulations. As human and historical formulations, it is of the very nature of the definitions of the Church to be *open to correction* and to stand *in need of correction*. Progress in dogma is not always necessarily just an organic development. Dogmas can even lead to a certain petrifaction of faith.[6]

Here, too, it seems proper to juxtapose John Henry Newman and Adolf von Harnack, as we have done several times. In his memorandum of 1888, Harnack concluded:

> Not exegesis and dogmatics, but the results of church historical research . . . will break . . . the traditions that confuse the conscience. Cardinal Manning once made the frivolous statement: "One must overcome history by dogma"; but we say, on the contrary: One must refine dogma by history.[7]

---

4. Newman, *Essay*, p. 64.
5. Cf. J.-H. Walgrave, *Newman the Theologian*, *pp.* 283–300.
6. Hans Küng, *The Council in Action: Theological Reflections on the Second Vatican Council*, trans. Cecily Hastings (New York, 1963), p. 205 (italics his).
7. Agnes von Zahn-Harnack, *Adolf von Harnack*, pp. 130–31.

Conclusion

Whether or not dogma is refined by history, it can be better understood through its history. Such understanding calls for history of at least two kinds. One is the specialized study in depth of a few doctrines in a few figures, as presented here. Another is the sort of comprehensive account of the development of Christian doctrine being undertaken by the author in his multivolume work, *The Christian Tradition: A History of the Development of Doctrine,* the first volume of which is to appear soon under the title: *The Making of the Catholic Tradition to A.D. 600.* Each has its place in scholarship. The full-length history without such studies as these can be accused of ignoring the nuances of development, while the samples apart from the framework of the total development can seem isolated. Yet within the context of the problem as we have set it, these samples may serve as an illustration of how Newman's *Essay on Development* (and, for that matter, Harnack's *Denkschrift*) are being vindicated by a research that goes beyond them and, in Ernst Troeltsch's phrase, "overcomes history with history."

Index

Index